THE BUGATTI STORY

*L'Ebé
Bugatti*

THE
BUGATTI
STORY

*Translated from the French
by Len Ortzen*

CHILTON BOOK COMPANY

Philadelphia · New York · London

Library of Congress Catalog Card Number 67-27858
Designed by Harry Eaby
Manufactured in the United States of America
by Quinn & Boden Company, Inc.

FOREWORD

This book was written in response to the long-felt desire of the Bugatti family to have a full and objective account of the life and work of Ettore Bugatti. It will also serve to correct the inevitable errors which have crept into various interesting publications on the subject during the past fifteen years in France and especially in other countries. All material used in this book has been carefully verified; and a special effort was made to collect the illustrations, many of which are here published for the first time.

My grateful thanks are due to Monsieur Louis Armand, who knew my father well, for kindly writing the preface.

I also wish to acknowledge the help given by the Bugatti Owners' Club in London, and especially by Mr. Hugh Conway, who kindly lent a number of photographs from his private collection, allowed me the use of material, and gave much valuable advice.

I am grateful to Monsieur Domboy, who worked with the "Guv'nor" from 1932 onwards and who is now assistant manager of the Molsheim works, for his personal recollections and his detailed information on Ettore Bugatti's railcars, yacht and numerous patents.

And I wish to express my admiration for Colonel Frédéric Loiseau, who made the adventurous journey across the Sahara in 1929, from Gao to Adrar, in a 1½-litre standard Bugatti.

PREFACE

By Louis Armand of the Académie Française

The material progress that man has achieved by the invention of new tools and techniques has been marked at each stage by men capable of transmuting into a concrete form the ideas and theories current at their time. These men can serve as examples to future generations, who must be prepared to act with the same determination and not just to continue the work of their predecessors. It is of great importance that they make the best use of all the possibilities offered by the world around them, create the new tools likely to widen man's horizons still further, and thus enrich the heritage handed down from one generation to another.

Ettore Bugatti was an outstanding example of this type of man, and our warmest thanks are due to Mademoiselle L'Ebé Bugatti for the book she has written on the life and work of her father.

The Molsheim car manufacturer might be said to have been the personification of his times, riding triumphantly the full tide of his era, during which hand-built cars gave way to mass production. His was the era which began a little before the turn of the century and which saw, resulting from the strange conjuncture of the internal combustion engine and pneumatic tires, the unexpected birth of horseless carriages which were faster than horses themselves.

People's minds were no more prepared for the scientific novelty of the period than they were for the literary. Those who were in favor of these new machines were "adventurers," in that they undertook the great task of innovators of all times. Urged on by their taste for adventure, they found a new impetus in the motor car; whereas the traditionalists, repelled by the noise and smell of these machines and by the dust they stirred up, condemned them out of hand.

It was during this period that Louis Renault's vocation was being formed, to the horror of his family. This vocation resulted from his love of speed and mechanics, a combination which is much more common nowadays. Although many people who like to drive fast have little knowledge of mechanics, it is nevertheless quite natural for these two inclinations to come instinctively, as anyone who has watched small children at play can confirm.

Both are accompanied and backed up by a love of risk. Building a car factory is a risk, and so is building a racing car. One risks one's life while testing it.

The danger inherent in this has been fully demonstrated by the blow dealt to two families of car manufacturers: Marcel Renault and Jean Bugatti were both killed while driving fast cars. But this risk is not only physical; it affects personal reputations, too, for during the period in question, car manufacturers looked upon their products as part of themselves and engaging the family name just as much as did their children. Fortunately, this tradition still exists in some firms, Peugeot in particular.

Ettore Bugatti was such a one, and the last to keep the flag of the artistically-built car flying high when the mass-produced car invaded the scene.

Bugatti maintained and vindicated the rule that quality production depended upon a small number of skilled workers and a small output. The time came when this rule was reversed. The skill of the motor mechanic was replaced by the skill of the machine worker; and it is now realized that quality rises proportionately to the number of cars produced, and is, therefore, a by-product of quantity.

It was inevitable that this "reduction" in manual skill should in the end submerge the craftsmen-produced cars. Ettore Bugatti was like the Cape-Horners who thought they could ignore steam. His was too strong a character to change to new methods, as others resigned themselves to doing. We must, however, do him the justice of admitting that the whole triumph of mass production really depends on the skills of *homo mecanicus,* which Bugatti so well served and promoted.

Just as masters of the great sailing ships had the satisfaction of opening sea routes for powered ships, for which the best school is still that of sail, so the workmen and foremen trained by Bugatti paved the way to mass production, which has given us quality mechanics. By his training, Ettore Bugatti raised his workmen to the level of artists and craftsmen. I think these two words would not have displeased him; they evoke his own personality. He always insisted that his engineers and technicians should never ignore the promptings of intuition.

When a connecting rod was being designed, he liked it to be modeled on the form and curves of a horse's humerus, for the family tradition of animal sculpture was never very far from the master's mind. In this respect the Molsheim school took quite a different line from most other workshops, where draftsmen worked conscientiously along the lines taught in technical schools and put their trust, above all, in calculations.

It was because his reputation extended beyond the motoring world that Ettore Bugatti was brought in to improve rail travel. In order to shake up the somewhat set ways of the French Railways—an otherwise fine service—two railway chiefs of the time, Raoul Dautry and Eugene Mugniot, decided to commission Bugatti to construct a new type of rail locomotion. I was a young engineer at the time, and thus came to know him. Although our training could not have been more different, I think I can claim that, during our collaboration, there sprang up between us a mutual esteem, based on a common respect for experience and a common love of engineering. For my part, like so many others, I fell under the spell of his charm and his singleness of purpose, for what he sought was technical truth rather than commercial considerations.

An example of this is his estimation of the comparative strain on engines caused by road and rail travel. At the time, it was thought that roads caused greater strain than the railway, with its smooth surface and easy gradients. Bugatti soon saw that the contrary was the case; that bends in roads brought a reduction in speed which eased the engine, whereas the unbroken high speed of a train imposed a constant strain. He was, of course, quite right, and instead of treating it as of small importance, he decided to overcome it by giving his railcars much greater power than had previously been customary. He thus showed the way to (mechanical) wisdom, and since then has been generally followed.

The result was that Bugatti railcars first ran to Deauville and then on the P.L.M. (Southern) line, enabling Paris businessmen to go to Lyons and back in one day, for the first time. This was a preface to the post-war network of rail and air services which give France a compact, centralized structure, typical of the "geographical contraction" of our day. Formerly, this was seen only in Switzerland, where good communications closely linked the chief towns—Basle, Berne, Zurich, Lausanne, Geneva.

In short, Ettore Bugatti's bold vision and genius opened the way in this field of communications, too. I and others with me were proud and happy to have been associated with him, sharing his faith in mechanics and, thereby, in human endeavor.

CONTENTS

PART ONE:

An Artist in Motor Cars

CHAPTER **1**

ETTORE BUGATTI
DISCOVERS MECHANICS

The title of this book could well have been *The Motor Car as a Fine Art*—a somewhat startling title in an age when car manufacture has become one of the biggest industries in the world. Ettore Bugatti foresaw this, and was one of those who helped to make it possible. Yet to the end of his days he remained a figure of another age—an age in which the conveyor belt had not yet eliminated craftsmanship, when the search for the best was not subject to the demands of mass production, and when individual imagination could have free rein. It has been said that fundamentally Ettore Bugatti was an artist. The paradox is that he was an artist in a field which no one had considered to be artistic until he came on the scene, and in which he started to work just because he did not believe himself to be a true artist.

He, himself, was well aware of this two-way pull, which was later to prove so fruitful, as is shown by a fragment of autobiography which I happened to find:[1]

"In order to explain the strange development of my career," he began, "I must first describe my environment

(1) It was undoubtedly his wish to write the story of his life. The pages that have been found, dated a few months before his death, were written during convalescence after flu.

during my childhood and what my life was like as a youth."

At this point I should, perhaps, fill out the rather cursory details he gave of his family background. Ettore Bugatti was born in Milan on the 15th of September, 1881, and had a brother, Rembrandt, and a sister, Deanice. His parents later moved from Milan to Paris, and in both cities their houses were frequented by artists. A few of their names will suffice to show the kind of atmosphere in which the young Ettore grew up and which had so much influence upon him. Among them were Giacomo Puccini and Leoncavallo; Ricordi, the music publisher; Lillica, who was the librettist of most of Puccini's operas; Arturo Rietti, well known for his pastels; the sculptors Prince Paul Troubetzkoy, De Grandi and Ercole Rosa (Rembrandt's godfather); Giovanni Segantini, well known for his paintings of snow landscapes, who married Carlo Bugatti's sister; and finally, when he was in Paris, Leo Tolstoy, whose philosophy left a lasting impression on the family.

"In this environment," my father wrote, "I acquired the idea that art could not be learned, and that it was wiser not to persevere if only mediocre progress was made; but that in order to come to such a decision some courage and intelligence were necessary, to understand and to judge whether one was worthy of the art or not."

His own father, Carlo Bugatti, was born in Milan in 1855. He should have lived a century earlier for his powers to have been appreciated to the full, for he was a painter, sculptor, woodcarver and architect, and also made stringed instruments of his own invention, and developed a new style of furniture. Everyone called him "the young Leonardo" because of his energy and new ideas.

Early in life he acquired a deep philosophical outlook. His good nature led him into all kinds of indulgences—a most forgivable form of egoism. He was of medium build and very handsome; he had bright blue eyes which sparkled with intelligence and mischief, and his keen glance was intimidating yet winning at the same time. When still quite young he grew a beard which was silky and fair, and he developed a habit of stroking and twisting it. In later life it turned gray, then white, with a yellow stain from his ruminative pipe smoking.

He had stomach trouble at an early age and was treated with salts of San Pellegrino and started to wear flannel belts. But he could not bear too much restriction, and so conceived an entirely new style of dress. He had trousers made to come well above his stomach and right up to his shoulder blades at the back, supported by very short braces. The two upper parts let down like the flaps on workmen's overalls. Over this garment he wore a frock coat which fell straight to his knees; it had slit pockets at the sides, and the two-inch, upright collar was fastened under the chin by two glass buttons the size of hazel nuts; they were like cat's eyes set in gold, and were linked by a thin gold chain. The coat was normally made of fine grain cloth in a dark color, but was of silk cloth for the summer. Naturally, a garment of such simple style had to be made by a good tailor, for there was no possibility of redeeming a mistake in its cutting. The task was far from easy, and was the cause of many a row! A black, low-crowned silk hat with a flat brim edged with corded ribbon for "dress" occasions, or the same kind of hat in a fine straw for everyday wear, completed his outfit.

He studied first at the Milan art school and later at the Académie des Beaux-Arts in Paris. After trying to apply his ideas on new shapes to architecture, he turned to cabinet-making and created a new style, or rather a new method of working. He exhibited his furniture and carvings, models and architectural designs in England, France and Italy.[1] He had a studio in Paris, so his children were educated in France

(1) He won many prizes and medals. Among them were: London Exhibition, 1888—diploma for fine furniture; Paris World Exhibition, 1900—silver medal; Turin Exhibition—first prize.

more than in Italy. About 1910 he settled in Pierrefonds, near the forest of Compiègne, the climate being more suitable for his wife's delicate health; and there he continued to paint.[1]

During the First World War he was mayor of Pierrefonds, and people still remember his work for refugees and the wounded. Even when the German advance was threatening the town, he had the temerity to carve a German spiked helmet with a Gallic cock perched triumphantly on it, wings outspread and clutching it with strong claws. He left this model quite openly in his studio, merely covering it with a damp cloth to keep it moist.

He died at Molsheim in April, 1940, on the eve of another invasion of France.

Carlo Bugatti and his environment had a great influence on his two sons, especially on Ettore, who learned from him to regard art as a flowering of one's personality and not as a means of earning money. Ettore also learned that artistic effort is of no use unless one is gifted, and that everything is justifiable in an artist except mediocrity. This was the cause of his change of ambition quite early in life.

"My first ambition was to be a great artist," he wrote, "and so earn the right to bear a name distinguished by my father.

"My brother, who became the greatest Bugatti of our line, had an eminent sculptor, Ercole Rosa, as a godfather. He was born with a very large head, which made Rosa say that he would become a great man or nothing at all; and in order to help on his destiny Rosa advised giving him the name Rembrandt.

"As the elder I had begun to study painting, sculpture and architecture. I really tried very hard to be an artist in the real sense of the word and not a builder in reinforced concrete,

(1) In 1910 he exhibited a very fine portrait at the Salon de Peinture in Paris. He was one of the judges at the Salon d'Automne and a member of the Société Nationale des Beaux-Arts.

who has a greater talent for handling figures than producing shapes. I had the best possible teachers in painting and sculpture, especially our family friend, Prince Troubetzkoy, the quality of whose works was well known.[1]

"But then my brother suddenly took to drawing. I saw at once, and confided in my dear mother that he was the true Bugatti and would soon be far better than I, in spite of my studies, even if he were not already. I told her, too, that two Bugattis in the same class might lead to confusion, and that under the circumstances I preferred to give up art.

"If a man has enough foresight to make such a decision, he ought to thank God for it.

"Rembrandt wanted to be an engineer and build locomotives. I wanted to be an artist, but I was no more gifted for art than he was for mechanics. In fact, without any preparation or advice, he was already making good progress in the career which I had embarked upon.

"One day, some friends of my father asked me to try out a motor-tricycle which had been built a year after the appearance of the De Dion tricycle. It had been made by the firm of Prinetti and Stucchi. Prinetti was an engineer and Stucchi a very good industrialist, one of the best at that time, 1895.

"In a short while, just by looking at the machine, I had grasped all the intricacies of its mechanism. I should add that my father attached great importance to his two sons being able to work with their hands, and a cabinetmaker's work is the best of groundings for mechanics.

"Even in establishments of higher education, manual work would be of great value to those who are choosing a career, whatever that may be. It is a relaxation and at the same time exercises muscles and brain.

"I very quickly thought of modifications that could be made to the tricycle; some of them proved to be valid, and

(1) Paul Troubetzkoy, born at Intra, on Lake Maggiore, in 1863.

my ideas were nearly always considered by the engineers responsible for building it.

"I was taught how to use materials to the best advantage by a kindly man who saw everything very clearly, and his advice was the best teaching I could have had. He examined things keenly and judiciously and his judgment was clear and unchallengeable. I often thought to myself that he was full of years and experience, and how happy I should be if I could ever know as much as he did. . . ."

In order to understand the young man's wholehearted enthusiasm, one must think of the attitude to road vehicles during the closing years of the last century. "It was a time when people were awakening to the possibilities of self-propelled road vehicles," he wrote, "and I was immediately fascinated by these new machines." None of the people who were working on mechanical road vehicles at that time was in fact motivated by thoughts of commercial gain. Nor was it really an economic need. As an early motoring correspondent, W. F. Bradley, wrote: "It was an aspiration to greater freedom, to an emancipation from the ties which bound man to the earth. The coming of the railways had not roused the same enthusiasm because they had been commercialized from the beginning, and because their object was to transport crowds of people, thus making no contribution to individual freedom, which the motor vehicle promised to do."

For Ettore Bugatti there was the added, the main, attraction of having something to create, to model, to perfect, and the joy of seeing the machine come into being, as a work of sculpture did in the hands of his father or his brother. He who never had any training in engineering—perhaps because he had none—found in mechanics a new dimension. This revelation changed the whole course of his life. With the same determination he had shown when he gave up the "fine arts," he threw himself into this entirely new kind of art, where so much was still to be invented.

"I could drive a motor-tricycle without knowing anything about its construction," he wrote. "Signor Stucchi, seeing that I was interested in this means of locomotion, asked my father to allow me to go to his factory. This was granted, although I had some difficulty in making my father understand that I should very much like to be an unpaid apprentice in that firm."

Indeed, Carlo Bugatti was quite unprepared for such a scheme, which seemed completely outside his own world. But he may have thought of his own father, Luigi, who had also been interested in science and architecture. In the mid-nineteenth century, Luigi Bugatti had sculpted monumental chimney-pieces which were much admired for their elegant form, but he had also poured all his money into solving the secret of perpetual motion.

So one day in 1898, the seventeen-year-old Ettore left his art school to become an apprentice in a motor-tricycle workshop in Milan.

CHAPTER 2

MOTOR-TRICYCLE RACES

On the 24th of May, 1899, an excited crowd was gathering on the Suresnes Bridge in Paris and along the road out to Versailles, in spite of the heat and the dust, to watch seventy-eight vehicles assembling for the start of a race. There were two-, three-, and four-wheeled vehicles, all with thin spokes and narrow tires. The drivers, wearing leather jackets or fur coats, were perched on high seats at extraordinarily long steering columns. The machines were square-shaped and stood high on their wheels, and had headlamps like lanterns and long copper bulb-horns, so that most of them looked like carriages that had lost their horses. They had, indeed, lost them forever. These tottery, clumsy, heroic vehicles were the first motor cars.

All over Europe at that time, these contraptions which appear almost prehistoric today but whose speeds then seemed terrifying, were taking part in competitions to test their qualities. On that particular May morning the cars were lining up for the Paris-Bordeaux race, and among them were the best and latest models in the world.

Some of the most famous drivers of the time were there too —Charron, Girardot, Edge, Jarrott, de Knyff, Osmont, Tart, and others. Forty-one of the entries were in the four-wheeled class and thirty-seven in the cyclecar and tricar class. Prob-ably few of the spectators noticed a slim, fair, rather frail-looking young man. He was not quite eighteen years of age, and had come with his tricar from Milan to take part in the race, alone, without helpers or supporters. He was Ettore Bugatti.

This decision to make the journey and take part in the race is evidence of his early development and bold nature, as well as of the great self-confidence which he retained to the end of his days. He had been working for barely a year with Prinetti and Stucchi, and had had no previous experience or mechanical knowledge. This tricar was the first he had made. (No model of it that can be positively identified has ever been found.) But his passion for racing was at once aroused, a passion he was never to lose; it was not so much for the race itself but because that was the natural complement of his passion for mechanics. Racing constituted the inexorable testing-bench without which all mechanical inventions remain abstractions; it alone could decide all problems, and was the indispensable, true test.

However, there is little to be learned from his writings about his first attempts at racing. In his fragment of autobiography he merely noted with characteristic reserve:

"Working in this factory (Prinetti and Stucchi) enabled me to get permission to build *the first twin-engine tricycle*. I took part in ten races with this first machine of mine and won all of them except one, when I was second.

"The best of these races, the one which gave me most satisfaction, was at Turin. I beat Gaste and Rigal, who had come from Paris to beat me. Even before the start, I was sure of winning.

"In the Paris-Bordeaux race I averaged fifty miles an hour and was running second, twenty minutes behind Osmont, when I ran out of petrol and had to give up (damaged fuel-tank)."

For more information about these early successes, one has to refer to the newspapers and motoring journals of the time. The earliest mention is dated March 1, 1899. Ettore, then aged seventeen and a half, took part in the Nice-Castellane race driving a De Dion-Bouton tricar of 1¼ HP.

On March 12th he was driving in the Verona-Mantua event of one hundred miles. Eighteen tricars took part, and Ettore Bugatti won on a Prinetti tricar fitted with a De Dion-Bouton engine. Count Biscaretti was second, and Fraschini third. In the motor-car class, victory went to Agnelli, driving a Fiat.

The Turin race, which Ettore referred to as 'the best of them,' was almost certainly the one on May 8th of the same year. It was over fifty-six miles, starting from Pignerol. He finished first of the forty-two entries, driving a tricar with a De Dion 1¾ HP engine.

Six days later he was taking part in the 109-mile Padua-Trevise race, but driving a different type of vehicle (of which more mention will be made later). It was a quadricycle, and his time of 4 hours, 35 minutes was the fastest in the race.

On September 11th he was second in the tricar class in a race from Brescia to Verona and back, a distance of 139 miles. But on September 28th he had to drop out of a race at Trevise because of a breakdown, after being third in a two-mile handicap sprint.

He had to drop out of the Paris-Bordeaux race, too, as he, himself, noted. But in this long and hard race, where he was entirely on his own, he showed what he was made of. He was competing against more experienced drivers, was jolted and shaken by potholes and met clouds of dust from other entries, many of which were more powerful than his own vehicle; yet he reached Poitiers third out of the thirty-seven entries in his class. On the following day, however, his tricar, No. 66, failed to arrive in Angoulême, the end of the next stage. According to W. F. Bradley, he had hit a dog and the damage to the tricar had proved impossible to repair. Charron won the race in the major class, driving a Panhard-Levassor, and Osmont was first of the tricars.

These early races and the experience gained from them had a great effect on the young Bugatti. He wrote of this himself, and explained how his career began to take shape.

"I regarded the tricar as a test-machine to be constantly altered and developed, and racing it to be the means of judging modifications, of deciding whether they should be retained or discarded.

"Meanwhile, I was studying the different types of engines being used at the time, examining their qualities and discussing their defects. And I determined to build a car of my own. As soon as I obtained permission, I designed it and got it built.

"The car was quite small but had four engines—two in front and two behind the rear axle.[1]

"I was not very happy about it, but tests were quite encouraging, nevertheless; and I decided to build a second car. But Prinetti and Stucchi refused to have it made, saying that they intended to concentrate on the manufacture of cyclecars.

"I had realized by then that I was completely taken by mechanics, in which I could clearly see so many imperfections. My ideas gave me no rest. I had time to reflect and think over my projects, and I suddenly found that I was left to my own devices. (The same thing happened several times in later life.)

"In the end, I decided to get down to designing my car first, and to plan the assembly of it later. I received a pleasant surprise toward the end of the summer of 1900, when the Gulinelli brothers asked me to join them. My father kindly agreed to participate in a small way, although he had little faith in the success of my undertaking.

(1) It was for this car that Pirelli made pneumatic tires for the first time. Their dimensions were those of the present "balloon" tire, 650 mm. x 120 mm.

"In October I began making the wooden models which were needed for the casting of the various parts at the foundry. And in the early months of 1901 my second car was ready for the road.

"It was a real triumph. I think it must have been the first light car. The 4-cylinder engine was water-cooled, and had a bore and stroke of 90 mm. x 120 mm. It had chain drive, four forward gears and one reverse. Ignition was by electric tube or magneto.

"The engine had overhead valves, and I believe I was the first to build engines with this feature. The car could easily reach a speed of forty mph. on the road. An important detail, for that time, was that each pair of valves could be instantly dismantled by the removal of a single nut. The car weighed about thirteen hundredweight."

There exists a contemporary account of this third vehicle made by Ettore Bugatti, which was to prove of great importance to the course of his career. In the issue of the *Gazzetta dello Sport* of Milan dated May 10th, 1901, there appeared the following article under the title *Ettore Bugatti's Car* and simply signed "E. V."

"For some time now, having a passion for cars and this new sport which interests so many lively minds in quest of better things, I have been following the development and the improvements in the building of engines.

"Yesterday was a great day for me, for it marked the success of a dear friend, Ettore Bugatti, who has built a quite magnificent car by his own efforts, without any help at all. I have been following his patient experiments for the past ten months, so am happy to record his triumph.

"Bugatti is very well known in the motoring world. The son of an artist, he, himself, is an artist to his very being. He served his apprenticeship by making and racing tricars. He loved his machine; he carried out modifications to it every day, in his workshop, until his tricar carried him victoriously over the finishing line of the races he entered.

"But the four-wheeled car, the fast car, was what he dreamed about. He studied the different types of engines, noticed their defects and thought about modifications, seeing the perfect car in his imagination. But he lacked the material aid to build it. Bugatti's gay disposition and his love of practical jokes did not inspire much confidence in him, and no one was prepared to invest in his capabilities as a car builder.

"So he began to put down on paper, in drawings and designs, all the ideas that his head was full of; and the pads of paper on which he spent whole days designing his car in every detail were soon encroaching on the space in his father's studio. Bugatti showed them to me on many occasions, explaining the workings of his car. He talked about it with such enthusiasm that it seemed to be speeding along at forty miles an hour even then. I sometimes feared that it might turn his mind.

"Among his many friends are the two Count Gulinellis, two brothers, of Ferrara.[1] They recognized a hidden brilliance in him, and were prepared to go into partnership with him to enable him to build his car. So last October he began making the wooden models, from his drawings, for the casting of the various parts.

"A month ago, after the 'Tour of Italy,' I went back to see Bugatti accompanied by the Chevalier Ricordi[2] and Georges Berteaux. The car was nearing completion, and Berteaux went into raptures over it. He predicted a great

(1) Bugatti was often invited to stay with them on their huge estate outside Ferrara, and it was there that he first became keen on horses and riding. (Author's note.)

(2) The music publisher. (Author's note.)

success abroad as well as at home, and arranged there and then to buy the first car of that type produced.

"Two days ago, Bugatti fitted the wheels, installed the provisional ignition system, and took the car out for its first trial run. It went superbly, reaching speeds of forty mph. But the engine is so powerful that, with a higher gear ratio, a much higher speed could easily be attained. Although it is a light car, it should not be confused with a 'voiturette.'

"It has a four-cylinder engine with electric ignition tubes. A completely new device is that each pair of valves can be dismantled by unscrewing a single nut. The engine and transmission and the rest of the mechanism are mounted on a rectangular steel chassis of maximum rigidity. Any kind of coachwork can be built on it, so well arranged is it all.

"Yesterday, this courageous and enterprising young man (he is only nineteen) received warm praise from the most qualified people in the motoring world. He is now the builder of a model which has already reached a high degree of perfection. The car he has constructed will be a happy reminder of his anxieties and weariness and long efforts.

"Bugatti, in partnership with the Gulinelli brothers, intends to open a big car factory in Milan."[1]

The first International Motor Show was being organized in Milan that year, 1901, and the City Council had given a silver cup for the best Italian model. Young Bugatti, full of confidence, decided to enter his new car.

"The competition was very severe," he wrote. "The members of the organizing committee and of the Automobile Club included some highly qualified motorists. A car test was organized. Lancia drove the Fiat."

(1) This fine project had to be shelved, because of the death of one of the Gulinellis. In the meantime, the De Dietrich firm bought the licence to build this car, and so drew the young Bugatti to Alsace. (Author's note.)

He would let no one but himself put the car through its paces. It was his from start to finish; he had been responsible for, or had supervised, the whole construction, from the drawing-board to final assembly. So he took the wheel for the car tests, and could not have been more successful. The car easily reached speeds of forty mph., which he considered could still be bettered.

The judges were quite as much impressed by the youth of the car's creator as by the excellent performance of its engine, but after several days had still not given their decision. Ettore grew tired of waiting, and went off to Lake Maggiore to join a lovely girl whom he had known since childhood, Barbara Mascherpa Bolzoni.[1] She became his wife not long afterwards. When he returned to Milan he found that he had won the Grand Prix[2] and had been awarded a special medal by the French Automobile Club.

(1) Ettore and Barbara were born the same year; their mothers were old friends, and sometimes the fancy took them to exchange babies for a while.

(2) Grand Prix, Milan International Exhibition, 1901, under the patronage of the Association of Lombardy Journalists. The handsome silver cup with a decorative panel of enameled allegorical figures is in the possession of Roland Bugatti.

CHAPTER 3

FIRST CONTRACT
AT NINETEEN

At nineteen, Ettore Bugatti was a well-built, healthy-looking young man with clear-cut features and of slightly more than average height. He had a rather long nose and deep blue eyes which were full of intelligence and kindness. His shapely mouth had a ready smile, revealing fine, white teeth; his rather full lips indicated a love for the good things of life, yet with his high, wide forehead and chestnut hair—soon to start thinning—he gave the impression of being a thoughtful, clear-minded man. A strong-willed, dimpled chin completes the portrait of this lively, fine-drawn face. His hands were a distinctive part of him, vigorous yet controlled in their gestures, like all the movements of his refined person.

Such was the elegant young man, with a touch of the dandy about him, who returned home from Lake Maggiore. Awaiting him was not only the Grand Prix but also one of the directors of the De Dietrich firm in Niederbronn, twenty-five miles from Strasbourg.

"He was very interested in my ideas and construction," Ettore wrote. "He said that Baron De Dietrich would like to see the car, and asked me if I felt inclined to go to Niederbronn. The idea and the journey appealed to me—to travel through Switzerland and see new regions. I set off without any passport or papers—travel was free of all formalities in those happy days. . . ."

On his arrival, things moved quickly. Baron Eugène de Dietrich was impressed with the Italian's intelligence and energetic mind, and after a few weeks, convinced of his mechanical genius, offered the young Bugatti a contract for the manufacture of his car under licence. As he was still a minor, the proposition had to be submitted to his father for approval and signature—surely a unique situation in the history of the motorcar industry.

The letter sent to Carlo Bugatti was as follows:

De Dietrich and Company,
Niederbronn, 26th June, 1902

Mr. Bugatti senior,
13, Via Marcona,
Milan.

Dear Sir,

As your son, Mr. Ettore Bugatti, is not yet of age, we are sending for your approval the agreement we made with him this morning concerning the production of motorcars of the type that Mr. Ettore Bugatti has designed and built. The terms are as follows.

We agree to pay Mr. Bugatti the following royalties on the sale of cars made to his design:

400 Frs. on each 10 HP car.

500 Frs. on each 15 HP car.

2,000 Frs. on each racing car, when the sale price is above 20,000 Frs. If the price of these racing cars is below this amount we will pay him ten per cent of the difference.

In addition, we will pay Mr. Bugatti the sum of 50,000 Frs. by installments, as follows:

19,000 Frs. immediately, for his car.

11,000 Frs. when he comes to work here, bringing with him all his designs, models, etc., for the racing car.

6,666 Frs. when the 15 HP car is completed and ready.

6,666 Frs. when the 10 HP car is completed and ready, and the remainder of the 50,000 Frs. when the omnibus is completed.

The acceptance of these terms binds Mr. Ettore Bugatti for a period of seven years, renewable by agreement, to give us all improvements and modifications he may make in the construction of his model, provided they do not constitute an entirely different type of car from the racing car which he has shown us.

In addition, Mr. Bugatti agrees to give us first refusal for the production of any car invented or assembled by him which is completely different from the present model.

Mr. Bugatti agrees to supervise the execution of his designs and models, and the sound construction of the cars in our workshops.

The cars built to the Bugatti design will be known as the "De Dietrich-Bugatti" cars.

We have the exclusive rights to sell these cars in all countries except Italy.

Mr. Ettore Bugatti retains the exclusive rights for Italy, and we agree to supply him with the cars at the usual trade price, less the above-mentioned royalty and the usual commission allowed to all our sales representatives.

In return, Mr. Bugatti agrees neither to make nor sell these cars in any country outside Italy, and to meet our arrangements as to their sale price.

We should be glad to receive your acceptance of these terms, and ask you to be good enough to have your son put his signature on your reply, and he will agree to keep to the contract after he attains his majority.

Yours faithfully,

De Deitrich and Company.

The contract, as can be seen, was of some importance. But the comments which Ettore Bugatti made on it in his unfinished autobiography are more revealing of the spirit in which he signed the contract and of his attitude to life.

"I received twenty-five or thirty thousand francs when

Ettore Bugatti at the work-bench in 1904, making parts for one of his first cars. (*L'Année Automobile*)

Bugatti's quadricycle, probably similar to the tricycle he built previously. Now in th Turin Automobile Museum. (*Mlle. Bugatti*)

Bugatti at the wheel of the car he built in 1898. (*Mlle. Bugatti*)

At the drawing board. (*L'Année Automobile*)

Bugatti and Mathis in the Paris-Madrid car.
(*Mlle. Bugatti*)

Bugatti in 1900.
(*L'Année Automobile*)

Bugatti at the wheel of his car for the Paris-Madrid race (1903), after the seating had been modified to give better visibility. It had been refused permission to start in its original form. (*Mlle. Bugatti*)

I handed over my designs," he wrote. "I was happy to have money to spend which I had earned myself; but this satisfaction is something I now find impossible to understand.

"I drew satisfaction, though, from being able to support myself without anyone's help and without being on the staff of some firm and paid for my work as I did it, and I found satisfaction in receiving a sum of money for a completed job of work which had given me pleasure to think out and do—which had even been fun to do—and which left me free at the end of it.[1]

"I have built many models since that time, and many of my inventions have fallen into the public domain. When I took out patents it was not to benefit financially from any infringements, but merely to make sure of not impairing the claims of other inventors, and to be quite sure that what I invented belonged to me. My patents result from my own work, and I am happy when I can improve on something already existing and arrive at a point which others have not yet reached.

"At one time—I think it was between 1905 and 1908—I had applied for, and been granted, more patents in Germany than anyone else.

"This profusion of new mechanical things was facilitated by circumstances which I will explain. It is my belief that the best way of developing one's ideas is to put them down on paper, to get them on the drawingboard. This is a great help in seeing what can be done.

"Powers of observation are indispensable in order to produce anything. Perhaps I can better explain what I mean by referring to the arts. Leonardo da Vinci had wonderful

(1) He designed five other types of cars for the De Dietrich firm, one being a racing car for Paris-Madrid (overhead camshaft engine, two valves per cylinder, B/S 160 mm. x 160 mm.) built under his supervision by the Société Alsacienne de Constructions Mécaniques at Graffenstaden.

powers of observation; he could reproduce with exactitude something which today we would take a magnifying glass to; he could catch movement as the camera does now, and at the same time he gave the illusion of life to his sketches, something that photography is unable to do.

"It is by observation that one can penetrate into the nature of things. If a man like Leonardo became a military engineer, he would be an expert at it; his advice on any subject would be invaluable, and his ideas on the matter would be highly original.

"An artist of this class misses nothing; the smallest detail, invisible to ordinary people, is enough to enable him to fix his subject. This habit of observation leads to the heart of the matter in all branches of human activity.

"I have said all this to try to show that observation is at the base of all progress and improvements in mechanics.

"Faster progress would be made in all fields if conceit did not cause us to forget or disdain the work done by others before us. There is a tendency to believe that nothing worthy of note has been done in the past, and this has an unfortunate bearing on our judgment; thus the present trend toward mediocrity, not because it would cost more to do better but because we do not know how to do better.

"The improvements I have made to mechanical constructions have resulted from such habits of observation. The drawingboard enables me to see in completed form whatever it is that I am about to make, but I often think that one should not put pencil to paper before having visualized what one wants to do from all angles. Over the years and after much experience in drawing quite novel and complicated things in pocket-books, I have come to work by a series of mental images; and the drawing board enables me to give effect to those images. A technician who cannot put down his ideas on paper is at a great disadvantage.

"To sum up, then—powers of observation and great facility with the pencil are the two attributes that matter most."

The first consequence of the contract with Baron De Dietrich was that Ettore Bugatti went to live at Niederbronn, and from that time on his home and work were to be in Alsace.

"I built a new model," he noted briefly, "which went into series production for a few years at the oldest metallurgic factory in Alsace-Lorraine, which thus became one of the first automobile factories in the world."

This model, which was almost certainly completed in 1902, is described by Hugh Conway[1] as a 4-cylinder 24 HP of 114 mm. bore and 130 mm. stroke, with a 4-speed gearbox and chain rear drive. The cylinders were cast in pairs, each pair being surrounded by a cylindrical aluminum casing acting as a water jacket.

The young car-builder took the wheel himself at an automobile meeting at Frankfurt on August 31, 1902. The sixth race was a handicap over 8 miles (12.87 km.), with four persons in each car. It was won by Goebel driving an 8 HP Bergmann from 2.3 miles (3.75 km.) handicap. Bugatti was second in a 20 HP De Dietrich from 275 yards, and Emil Mathis from scratch was third in the 24 HP De Dietrich.

In the next scratch race over 9.9 miles (16 km.), Bugatti was again second, this time to a 40 HP Mercedes. The motoring journal *Der Motorwagen*, however, printed the following comment on the race:[2]

"The entries in this event were a 40 HP Mercedes Simplex, a 16 HP Panhard-Levassor, a 16 HP De Dietrich and a 20 HP De Dietrich, and all the spectators thought it was a ridiculous race because the winner was bound to be the 40 HP Mercedes, unless an accident occurred. But a very different aspect is given to the result when the speeds of the four cars are compared:

(1) *Bugatti,* by H. G. Conway, publ., Foulis, 1963.

(2) *Der Motorwagen,* September 15, 1902.

Mercedes Simplex	40 HP	68.48 km. p. h.
De Dietrich-Bugatti	20 HP	63.83 km. p. h.
Panhard-Levassor	16 HP	58.15 km. p. h.
De Dietrich-Turcat-Méry	16 HP	55.16 km. p. h.

"The real winner is thus seen to be the new De Dietrich-Bugatti, which with its 20 HP achieved almost the same performance as the Mercedes with its 40 HP!

"Oddly enough, the spectators were clearly conscious of this throughout the race and cheered Bugatti, who showed every sign of being a first-class driver, each time he passed the stands. Even the officials left their places to get as close as possible to the bends, to see the masterly manner in which Bugatti took them every time."

This press report is believed to be the first time Ettore Bugatti was mentioned as driving a racing car bearing his name. A fortnight later he celebrated his twenty-first birthday.

A LETTER FROM BARON DE DIETRICH

The qualities of the cars which Ettore Bugatti designed for the Niederbronn firm can be judged from the following letter written to the young engineer by Baron Eugène de Dietrich in 1909.

Dear Mr. Bugatti,

I understand from Mr. Pétri that you would like me to give you a certificate on your cars, which we have been using for several years. It gives me great pleasure to confirm that your cars have always given us complete satisfaction in every way. The four cars, a tourer, two big limousines and a coupe, all of your 1903 35 PS type, have each done more than 62,000 miles and are still in perfect condition. The oldest of them, the tourer, was entirely overhauled after doing about 120,000 miles, and the chief parts were found to be in perfect working order; apart from a few brass bearings, nothing needed replacing. Special mention must be made of the steering box, which still shows hardly any wear.

The good use we have had from your cars is confirmed by many of our customers who have been driving your cars for years. All agree that they are robust and sturdy, and quite a number of their owners who have since bought more modern cars have often had occasion to regret their old Bugatti, which never let them down.

Yours sincerely,

(signed)   Baron Eugène de Dietrich.

P.S. One of the Verkehrstruppen cars of Metz arrived here a day or two ago for repairs. It was said that of all the different types in use, yours is the most robust and sturdy.

It is interesting to compare this letter with one written to Ettore Bugatti ten years later by Dominique de Dietrich, Eugène's son. The car referred to was apparently one of the first to be built at Molsheim.

Dear Mr. Bugatti,

In reply to your letter, I am pleased to say that the car you delivered to me in 1911 is still giving excellent service and has done about 125,000 miles without any major repairs being required.

It is a very pleasant car to drive and holds the road well. The engine is very sturdy, most efficient and reliable, and it has never given any trouble even on the steepest hills; neither have I noticed any signs of overheating in the hottest weather, and at all times it has run very smoothly.

Although it is a small car and economical on petrol and oil, I have seen it overtake and leave much more powerful cars behind.

In short, I have nothing but praise for your car, and am glad to tell you how highly I think of it. I have never hesitated to recommend it to my friends.

Yours, etc.,

(signed)   Dominique de Dietrich.

CHAPTER 4

A CAR IN A CELLAR

One of the great sporting events of this heroic period in motoring history was expected to be the Paris-Madrid race which was organized in 1903. Bugatti designed a car for the De Dietrich firm especially for this race, a 50 HP which had a 4-cylinder engine and chain transmission, like his previous models, but with a daring novelty: the driving seat was over the rear axle and set very low. It would be considered quite normal today, but at that time the usual practice was for the driving seat to be placed so high that the driver's knees were at least on a level with the bonnet. However, Ettore suffered his first setback through thus being in advance of his time; the race officials refused to authorize the car to start because of the lack of visibility for the driver. Modifications were later carried out to bring the seat forward and higher. As for the Paris-Madrid race, so many fatal accidents occurred that the authorities stopped it at Bordeaux.

The following year, 1904, Bugatti built another model for the De Dietrich firm (4-cylinder engine of 130 mm. x 140 mm.; the cylinders were cast in pairs, each having a copper water jacket) which seems to have existed in two versions —one of 24 to 28 HP and another of 30 to 35 HP. However, not long afterwards, the De Dietrich firm stopped making cars and young Bugatti found himself free to make other arrangements.

"I was hypnotized, drawn more and more to the mechanics of motors," he wrote. "These exciting problems had me completely under their sway, and so began for me the hard uphill task, the thankless labor of constructing and destroying and beginning again, without a break or rest, and for days, months, years even, until success finally rewarded all my efforts.

"I changed tactics and dropped light cars in order to make big ones, about 1904, for a company which had been formed to produce my cars under licence. This was at the Société Alsacienne de Constructions Mécaniques in Graffenstaden.

"One of these models was a 4-cylinder with dimensions of 140 mm. x 160 mm., and had two valves per cylinder operated by an overhead camshaft and curved tappets. This was my first use of curved tappets, which were later to contribute greatly to my resounding successes in races. Only a few cars of this type were built."

He was referring to a model named Hermes which was designed for Emil Mathis, who ran an export and import business at Strasbourg under the name of E. E. C. Mathis, and was also agent for the De Dietrich firm of Lunéville and Niederbronn,[1] and for Fiat of Turin. When De Dietrich ceased production, Mathis came to an arrangement with Bugatti.[2] It was in a room on the top floor of the Hotel de Paris, rue de la Nuée-Bleue, Strasbourg, that Bugatti designed this model. The hotel belonged to Mathis's father.

Bugatti's association with Mathis did not last long, but it enabled him to meet and become friendly with the man

(1) The De Dietrich house at Lunéville, near Nancy, was directed by Baron Turkheim and built Turcat-Méry cars under licence. It was independent of the Niederbronn branch, and continued its production when the other ceased.

(2) According to W. F. Bradley, Mathis had obtained the rights to sell De Dietrich cars in Italy, and he paid royalties to Bugatti on the cars produced at the SACM in Graffenstaden.

who was later to be his first collaborator and then a famous driver of his racing cars. This was Ernest Friderich, then a mechanic working for Mathis. More than forty years later, after Bugatti's death, Friderich recalled that early association with Bugatti in an article he wrote for *Bugantics,* the magazine of the Bugatti Owners' Club of Great Britain:[1]

"My work (at E. E. C. Mathis) consisted of tuning cars which we received from these firms (for whom Mathis was agent) before they were delivered to customers. Our garage included a hangar large enough to take six cars, while alongside it were some stables belonging to Monsieur Hyllé, of 54, Faubourg de Pierre, Strasbourg. Some time later, when the Dietrich firm at Niederbronn ceased production, Monsieur Bugatti came to an agreement with Mathis for the construction of an entirely new car. . . .

"The car was produced at Illkirch Graffenstaden and given the name 'Hermes.' I used to take a tram to get to the factory, which was about five miles outside Strasbourg, but Monsieur Bugatti went on horseback. Later, when he employed me full time, I built twenty-five chassis which were stored in the courtyard. One of them was bought by an American general, Costry Butt, and I drove him to the German Army maneuvers and also to the French Army maneuvers.

"It was in another of these cars that, in 1905 (1907?), I took part in the Kaiserpreis race at Hamburg and then in the Prince Henry Cup, with the Guv'nor driving and myself as riding mechanic. Afterwards, Bugatti and Mathis separated, and then Monsieur Bugatti asked me to work for him in a new venture. This car was built in a hangar which stood in a large garden about a mile from Graffenstaden; the Darmstadt Bank advanced the Guv'nor the money to buy the machinery needed for the construction of the car. Next to

(1) Friderich wrote the article in 1949 and it was first published in *Bugantics,* 12, 2 & 3.

the hangar and the workshop was the drawing office, where three draftsmen worked to the Guv'nor's instructions. There were three of us in the workshop too—a turner, a fitter, and myself. This was in 1906 and 1907.

"In July, 1907, the model was ready for the road, and its tests were highly satisfactory. After a few journeys to Cologne, to the Deutz Gas Engine Works there, that firm began to build the car under licence. Monsieur Bugatti was made manager of the production department, and went to live near the factory. It was then the end of August or beginning of September, 1907, and the last job I did was to dismantle the car, part by part, and deliver it to the drawing office. In October I left for Lunéville to start my military service, and spent the next two years in the Horse Artillery."

This model was a 50 to 60 HP, 4-cylinder of 150 mm. x 150 mm., with four-speed gearbox and chain drive.

"The engine," wrote Bugatti, "was the first, I believe, to have an overhead camshaft and with its four cylinders cast in a single block.

"It was the first time, too," he added, "that I agreed to take an appointment with a firm, whilst being remunerated by the royalties I received on the production of my car under license.

"I took with me, to this factory, the draftsmen who were in my employ and the mechanics who had assembled the model. Production was concentrated on a large car. I was in charge of the production of my car at the Deutz Works, but I had retained the right to work independently on any other project in which I might become interested."

These remarks are most revealing. Ettore Bugatti could well have been contented with his position in the firm; to be chief production manager, at twenty-three years of age, in a factory as large as the Deutz Gasmotoren Fabrik was no mean achievement. But he felt himself fettered by his "appointment" in the service of others. It is probably not too much to say that the most valuable clause in his contract, from his point of view, was the one allowing him to experiment on projects for his own account. In addition to this independence of spirit, his sense of loyalty to his associates was already showing itself. He retained this team spirit throughout his working life.

He designed another model for Deutz in 1909. This was a 13 to 25 HP, 4-cylinder of 92 mm. x 120 mm., giving a capacity of 3.2 litres; it had a four-speed gearbox and a shaft-driven overhead camshaft. Specialists consider it to be a "pure Bugatti." However, his mind was on something else. Making good use of the latitude allowed him, he designed a quite different model for his own account—a light car with an engine of 1,100 cc., weighing no more than six cwt and capable of fifty mph. on the flat.[1] Deutz was concentrating on producing big cars and were unlikely to be interested in this new model, so Bugatti decided to build it himself in his spare time. He worked patiently for many months, gradually assembling it in the cellar of the house where he was living in Cologne. When the car was completed he found he could not get it out of the cellar—the door was too narrow. So, helped by Friderich, who had just finished his military service, Bugatti took it to pieces and assembled it again in the open. And he gave it a name which later became renowned—*Pur-Sang*. This was the first "thoroughbred" from the Bugatti stable.

(1) The prototype (4-cylinder 8 valve, 62 mm. x 100 mm.) was in the small Bugatti "museum" at Molsheim until the Second World War.

CHAPTER 5

THE BIRTH OF MOLSHEIM

For several days in September, 1909, at Cologne, a young, thin-faced man could have been seen driving fast in a small car whose clean, slim lines gave it an appearance of unusual lightness. This driver was world famous—he was Louis Blériot, the aviator who had made the first flight across the English Channel just two months before. And the car was soon to become famous, too; it was Ettore Bugatti's *Pur-Sang*.

Cologne had organized an aviation meeting and had invited the celebrated flyer; and Bugatti, who was already French at heart, had offered him hospitality during his stay. Thus it happened that Blériot was almost certainly the first Frenchman to drive a pure Bugatti. He was using the small prototype each day to go to the airfield outside the town.

Blériot's enthusiasm for this new machine must have convinced my father that the important decision he had made was the right one—to set up in business for himself.

One day in December, 1909, he and Friderich got into the small car—which was called "the bathtub" because of the shape of its body—and drove to the Darmstadt Bank in Strasbourg. Bugatti had an appointment with Monsieur de Vizcaya senior, the banker, who had discovered an old dyeworks which might be suitable for a car factory. It was near a village called Molsheim, in Alsace, and could be rented quite cheaply. The three men went to have a look at it.

The buildings were fairly small but could be converted into workshops; there was a house nearby, and half of it was to let. The owner, a Fräulein Geisser, was prepared to let the buildings and half of the house for five thousand marks a year. Bugatti accepted there and then. He left Friderich to put the buildings in order and went to Paris and thence to Cologne to collect his wife and children.

At Christmas we all moved into the new home, where we were to live for the next thirty years, except for a few short interludes.

"On 25th January, 1910," Friderich informs us,[1] "the first machine-tools were delivered, and continued to arrive at the rate of two or three a week. At the same time I was getting together a nucleus of skilled workmen, turners and fitters, millers, smiths, and the like. When the workshops were fully equipped the draftsmen who had been with us at the Deutz factory came and joined us. Five cars were built and delivered to customers in 1910, and that year I started driving in races, though of course only on a small scale. . . ."

The whole character of the Molsheim works is revealed in the above lines: the artisanal manner and conditions, which were maintained in the best sense right until the peak period, and the close relationship with racing, which was considered the indispensable test-bench.

Five cars produced in a year . . . this, of course, is what strikes one most. The production rate soon increased considerably; yet even when Bugatti cars were famed the world over each one was still built, finished and tuned as though it were a unique model being made for a particular customer, and requiring the personal attention of its constructor. Such an attitude was by no means as rare at that time as it would be today; mass production was still unknown, and cars were hand-built for the most part, each an expression

(1) In his article written for *Bugantics* in 1949.

of a creator's personality. But probably none was as concerned as Bugatti to perpetuate this situation. Faced with the attractions of large-scale series production and lower costs, he retained his independent outlook, his freedom to invent, and his urge for perfection down to the smallest details. Production costs meant nothing to him, once he was set on an idea. He took little notice of trends among rival car manufacturers, and paid no more attention to the presumed tastes of the public.[1] It is all the more remarkable that the public followed his so often. Such was the case with the first type he produced at Molsheim.

"This was a very light car," he wrote, "and was greatly appreciated, selling very easily, especially in France. The engine was enlarged from 60 mm. bore to 65 mm. x 100 mm., but the general disposition of the cylinder block and the distribution was the same as now; in particular, the mechanism was given just as complete protection. The suspension had four semi-elliptic springs with many thin metal strips to increase flexibility. Fuel consumption was insignificant."

A car of this type gave a very good account of itself in the Gaillon hill-climb in October, 1910. Beside the big-cylinder cars, it had the appearance of a toy; a little gem, said some people. But, with Darritchon at the wheel, it took second place with a time of 1 min., 3.8 secs., and people at once began to take it seriously. W. F. Bradley wrote enthusiastically about it in *The Motor* a week or two later.[2] The following are extracts from the article:

"Those who estimate motorcar value on seating capacity and superficial area are not likely to become purchasers of

(1) For instance, despite many urgings, notably by his son, Jean, in later years, he never built cars with a left-hand drive.

(2) *The Motor,* November 1, 1910. This article, entitled *A New Light Car* and with the sub-heading *First Description of Another Light Car Having Some Striking and Original Features,* was undoubtedly the first to call attention to Bugatti cars.

the Bugatti. The designer of this little car, indeed, has made no attempt to compete with the low-priced popular models already on the market, the price of the Bugatti being higher than any other car of equal horsepower offered to the public. The reason is that the new production stands in a class by itself. M. Bugatti, an Alsatian designer (*sic*) with a high reputation in German factories, has sought to produce what may be termed the motorcar pony, but a pony that is fit to stand comparison with the most costly product of the best factories, and able, notwithstanding its small size and low power, to hold its own in the matter of speed with any touring car built.

"Frankly, we did not think it could, for, notwithstanding a surprising demonstration at the recent Gaillon hill-climb, the impression remained that these small, light cars generally hold the road badly at high speeds. Fully equipped, with mudguards, lamps, horn and all touring accessories, we made a demonstration run in the suburbs of Paris. After being warned twice that speeding was not allowed in the straight avenues of the Bois de Boulogne, we got into the suburbs of Paris, where fate sent us a big Benz Prince Henry car of 105 mm. by 165 mm. bore and stroke, four passengers, and pure touring body to act as pacemaker. The Prince Henry car was driven by a hot-blooded sportsman in his teens, who went over the most abominable roads between Paris and Saint-Germain at a speed only limited by the ability of his car to hold the road. Yet it was possible with the little Bugatti to keep within 50 yards of his pointed stern all the way, and with less discomfort than is experienced in many cars three times the size and weight. The makers guarantee that the little Bugatti can maintain 60 miles an hour and, although no opportunity was given of definitely proving this, the claim seems to be well founded.

"In city traffic the little car proved as remarkable as on the straight-away stretches for, being small, it could worm through where larger cars were held up; it was wonderfully quick in acceleration, absolutely silent on low gears, while the changes were made without a click being heard. . . ."

The reasons for the immediate success of the "little Bugatti" could not have been better stated. In May of the following year it again took second place in a hill-climb at Limonest; then on the 4th and 5th of June, at the Sarthe Meeting, it gained two first places, the drivers being Gilbert and the banker, De Vizcaya. However, its qualities were demonstrated in the most spectacular manner in the French Grand Prix of that year, 1911. Among the starters at Le Mans were a 6 litre "Savannah" type Fiat driven by Victor Hémery and a 4-cylinder De Dietrich (of 185 mm. x 160 mm.) with Arthur Duray at the wheel; an Excelsior which had taken part in the 1908 Grand Prix; two Rolland-Pilain cars with dimensions of 110 mm. x 165 mm., the drivers being Rigal and Gabriel; a big Cottin-Desgouttes, several much lighter cars, and the lightest of them all, an all-white 4-cylinder Bugatti of 65 mm. x 100 mm. (1,327 cc.). Ernest Friderich was at the wheel, and the car was so small that the riding mechanic had to hold the spare wheel in his arms because there was no place to attach it.

W. F. Bradley watched the race, and wrote a colorful report on it. The heat on that July day was overpowering, well up in the nineties; and as there was no shade on the roads, the pneumatic tires began to melt. At one stage, Hémery thought of retiring. Young Duray took advantage of the great thirst of his ancient De Dietrich to drench himself with water, too. The number of accidents soon began to mount. Maurice Fournier's front axle snapped in half, and he was killed. Other cars had their cylinders burst or their rear axles break, and drivers gave up one after the other. Only the imperturbable Friderich appeared in excellent form. "While the two-ton monsters were skidding around the hairpin bend opposite the stands, the little 6-cwt Bugatti slipped round without any apparent effort, without a trace of skidding, and without the driver changing gear. The contrast was so great that each time Friderich came round, a roar of applause rose from the spectators."

Hémery took first place, averaging 56.5 mph. over a distance of almost four hundred miles. Friderich was second, 51 minutes behind. Duray had dropped out of the race; the huge Cottin-Desgouttes had broken down. Among the few to finish were Gabriel, who had made a name for himself in the Paris-Madrid race, Leduc in a two-stroke Cote and the other Rolland-Pilain.

"The public," commented Bradley, "began to take notice of this new constructor of cars, whose business was only two years old, and that he knew more about the subject than the big firms whose fame had spread round the world."

In any case, the Molsheim business was growing larger. The twenty employees at the beginning had increased to sixty-five early in 1911. Friderich was constantly busy, supervising the finishing of the chassis, then doing the final adjustments and testing. Ettore Bugatti had built a new workshop, to have Friderich nearer at hand. There, with Friderich and three others, he assembled what proved to be one of the most popular Bugatti cars. It was a very light two-seater with bore and stroke of only 55 mm. x 90 mm. (855 cc.), and the 10 HP engine turned at 2,000 rpm. Friderich was sent to show it to the Wander firm at Chemnitz, in Saxony, and to Peugeot at Beaulieu, in the Doubs (Eastern France). The latter firm acquired the licence, and so was born the 'Baby' Peugeot.[1] Friderich drove the model to Aix-les-Bains to leave it with the firm's general manager, M. Gudorge, and returned to Molsheim by train. "As little time as possible

---

(1) By 1914 three thousand Baby Peugeots had been built. One of them is owned by Mr. C. W. P. Hampton, and is still capable of doing 40 mph. with a fuel consumption of 50 miles to the gallon.

had to be lost on these journeys," wrote Friderich, "so that production would not suffer."

Production was being concentrated on the 4-cylinder Type 13. Three chassis were built in February, 1911, and four in March and April. The number rose to six a month and then to eight by the summer. "The Guv'nor wanted nine in December," Friderich recalled, "to bring the total up to seventy-five for the year. And with hard work, goodwill and perseverance, we managed it. . . ."

A Letter to a Customer

The following letter gives an interesting insight into the kind of relationship which existed between Ettore Bugatti and his customers. Dr. Espanet eventually became one of his best friends.

Molsheim, 11th April, 1913.

Dear Dr. Espanet,

Your esteemed letter of the 5th inst., has been received and has given me much pleasure.

I am delighted to hear that my small car is giving you every satisfaction. I much regret being unable to supply you with a car which would meet the demands of as good a judge as yourself. In fact, I will not hide from you that as my small cars have to be sold relatively cheaply, it has not been possible to eliminate some minor inconveniences which would otherwise have made the car much more practical. From the point of view of construction, it is faultless; but some details are not as I should like them to be.

I am much obliged to you for having suggested to M. Garros that he should come to see me, and I shall be happy to discuss the matter of a bigger car with him.

I am building a few cars with bore and stroke of 100 mm. x 160 mm. I should like you to be a customer for one of them, if you are interested, and would give you special terms.

As for the 8-cylinder, it is on the drawingboard but not yet in production. The 8-cylinder car I mentioned to you will have an engine with 100 mm. bore, but the stroke has not yet been decided.

It will be larger than a Rolls Royce car, but lighter; with a closed body it will reach a speed of 100 m.p.h., and I hope to make it quite silent. When the first is on test I intend taking it on a long journey, and shall not fail to come and see you to have your opinion of it.

There is really no need to tell you that production of these cars will be very limited and their make faultless. Each one will be tested for at least 600 miles before delivery and will have a five-year guarantee. The car will be extremely dear, but will bear no comparison with any other of its kind.

If I succeed in getting what I am striving for, it will undoubtedly be a car and a piece of machinery beyond all criticism.

I should be delighted if you could come here, and I hope you will take advantage of M. Garros's journey and accompany him.

In the meantime, I remain, etc.,

E. Bugatti.

PART TWO:

The Guv'nor of Molsheim

CHAPTER **6**

FIRST SUCCESSES

The only way of realizing what the cars produced at Molsheim during those immediate pre-war years meant to early car enthusiasts is to refer to contemporary accounts. For instance, Gabriel Espanet, who had abandoned surgery for flying in 1907, recalled for me how he "discovered" Bugatti cars.

It was in 1910, at one of the first Motor Shows at the Grand Palais in Paris. Immediately to the left on entering, in a gallery, he noticed a name he already knew—Bugatti. Not that he had heard of the car builder, but oddly enough he had recently been to the Louvre and seen an exhibition of sculpture by Rembrandt Bugatti. He had taken a keen interest in the work of the young sculptor, so was all the more struck at coming across the same name in such different surroundings. He made his way to the stand, much intrigued.

"It was like seeing Nieuport's first aeroplane,"[1] he told me. "I found myself looking at a car completely different from the usual form of construction. I was so taken by the simplicity and harmony of its styling, as well as by the impression of power it gave, that even without a trial run I ordered one there and then. Ettore Bugatti was not at his stand that day,

(1) Edouard Nieuport, a well-known pioneer aviator, learned to fly in a monoplane he had built himself. It was to this revolutionary type of aircraft (for the times) that Dr. Espanet was alluding.

but I found him there when I went back the following day. 'What decided you to buy one of my cars?' he asked with curiosity. 'Did someone tell you about it?' 'No one at all,' I replied. 'Well, you're quite right!' he said with assurance."

Self-assurance was obviously one of his strongest features. But in the above incident it is difficult to know what to admire most—Bugatti's certitude as to the quality of his work or Dr. Espanet's perception in ordering the car of a young and unknown constructor, and exhibited for the first time, but which was in fact to gain victory after victory. For the car was the Type 13, mentioned in the previous chapter. Dr. Espanet's quick decision was all the more meritorious for the price was quite high—seven thousand marks for the chassis alone, delivered without any bodywork or accessories other than a revolution counter.

Dr. Espanet was so content with the car, however, that he told his friend Roland Garros, the famous pioneer aviator, about it; and a few months later Garros went to visit the Molsheim factory. His first impression was one of surprise. When he entered the gate, instead of the usual comings-and-goings of a car factory (even a small one), he saw Ettore Bugatti dressed for riding, with a Tyrolean hat, and walking a fine pony around the courtyard.

At that time, it is true, the Molsheim works had little resemblance to the traditional image of a factory. My father, having first rented the place, had soon become the owner and decided to make it the family home. My brother Jean had been born at Cologne on January 15, 1909. Then I had arrived, and been given the curious name L'Ebé; my father was so overjoyed at having a daughter that he thought up this name from his own initials. . . . Lydia was born after me, so there were three children in the family when we all moved to Molsheim, to the house and grounds which were soon to become the hub of the Bugatti world.

When Garros paid his first visit, the rural aspect of the

place—and the space given to horses—greatly overshadowed the industrial side, which was still in its early stages. Photographs taken at the time show large, well-kept paddocks and sleek, well-groomed horses, and . . . a small building in which were assembled the cars destined to become famous. Later on, the workshops gradually extended into the paddocks, and then some of the fields were turned into paddocks. The original workshop was converted into a coach-house and contained a magnificent collection of horse-carriages, nearly fifty of them, with a fine display of saddles and harnesses. Bugatti designed a set of harnesses for a four-horse team and had it made in his own workshops; it was of white leather, and the silver rings were given an ivory covering to keep the reins from becoming soiled.

Bugatti loved riding and kept a number of thoroughbreds. Many of his ideas and solutions of mechanical problems came to him while riding, though it was chiefly a means of relaxation. He would interrupt his riding and go to the workshops in riding breeches and top boots if he had suddenly found the reason for a car part not working properly. On other occasions, he would get astride an old bicycle or an electric runabout which he had made himself, and go through the grounds of his estate to the various workshops.

When Garros paid his first visit, Bugatti had just finished tuning a new racing car, and one of this type had already been delivered to the Duke of Bavaria, brother-in-law to the King of Belgium. Garros liked the look of the car so much that he ordered one then and there—which is why this type is sometimes called the "Garros." Only seven or eight of them seem to have been produced.

"The Guv'nor was always searching for new ideas," wrote Friderich, "and had secretly designed a car which was completely different from his previous types. It was a large car of 5 litre capacity, with a 100 mm. bore and 160 mm. stroke. Production was pushed forward, and the car was ready early in 1912. A great friend of the Guv'nor, M. Hylle, drove one of this type in the Herkhomer Cup Race (for owners only) and I was his riding mechanic. This road race through Germany and Alsace passed by Molsheim. Madame Bugatti had set up a buffet at the gates of the estate for the competitors, and it was a great joy for us to be able to pull up there. We had a glass of excellent champagne and some tasty sandwiches. At the end of the race we were declared the winner on points. That was one more success, and it was only a beginning. . . ."

Ettore Bugatti added that the car "naturally had an overhead camshaft engine," and that "for the first time I introduced my tri-valve arrangement—two small inlet valves and one larger exhaust valve. I later used this in all my 8-cylinder designs, and then in models of all my cars."

Garros's purchase of the car marked the beginning of a strong friendship with its manufacturer. During the next two or three years the French aviator made many visits to Molsheim, on two occasions flying there in his own aircraft and landing in the meadows near the workshops. Considering that Alsace was then part of Germany and that Molsheim was in a military zone, these landings appear most remarkable. But private air transport was so exceptional in those days that the regulations made no provision for it!

This was a particularly active and successful time for Bugatti, both in production and racing.

In 1911 or 1912 he built a special racing car with two of the normal 1.4 litre Type 13 engines coupled in tandem. This was the first 8-cylinder Bugatti, a fast car, which had relatively little success in races. It could reach 87 mph., whereas the 1911 Grand Prix car never did more than 66. Friderich drove the two-engined car in the Gaillon hill-climb of October, 1912, but failed to complete the course, the third gear change having broken halfway up the hill. A Bugatti (65 mm. x 100 mm.), however, won its class (under 1.4 litre, racing) in 53.5 seconds. Fastest time of all was made by Erle in a 200 HP Benz of 200 mm. x 250 mm., with 22 seconds.[1]

At the Whitsun Sarthe Meeting, Bugatti himself drove his "Garros" model and Friderich was at the wheel of a 1.4 litre. They won the three races which were held at Sillé-le-Guillaume, La Flèche and Laval, in that order.

At the Mont Ventoux hill-climb, also in 1912, Bugatti drove the same car and made fourth fastest time with 19 mins., 16.4 secs. for this 13¼ mile course (a new record of 17 mins., 46 secs. was made by Boillot in a Peugeot); while Friderich drove the 65 mm. x 100 mm. Bugatti and climbed in 27 mins., 14 secs.

"My small factory acquired greater importance," wrote Bugatti. "Production was increasing. The nights were often short, but orders were flowing in."

The name of Bugatti was, in fact, becoming renowned at many race meetings. Friderich has written of how he took part in numerous races—the Val-Suzon, Limonest-Lyon, Mont Ventoux-Avignon, Nancy, Toul, and others—and invariably gained first place. "All this traveling had to be done between Saturday and Monday morning, as I had to be at the factory during the normal working week. The tasks of testing and adjusting chassis absorbed all my time, often until late in the evening. The monthly output at the beginning of 1913 was 12 chassis, but the number increased month by month to reach 19 in December, making a total of 175 for the year. Work increased still more in 1914, and we produced 27 chassis in March, in addition to getting ready the racing car (100 mm. x 180 mm.) which I was to drive in the Grand Prix at Indianapolis on May 30, 1914."

Bugatti had decided to try his luck in this great international event of 500 miles, where he would be competing

(1) According to C. W. P. Hampton, another Bugatti driven by Tonello won the under 1.4 litre touring class in 58 secs., the fastest touring class competitor being an Hispano-Suiza of 80 mm. x 100 mm., in 43 secs. This course was on the main highway between Vernon and Rouen.

against the most powerful cars of Peugeot and Delage. To this end, he built a special version of his 5 litre "Garros." It had a lengthened stroke, from 160 to 180 mm., and a conventional rear axle in place of the chain drive.

A quarter of the way through the race, Friderich was in the lead. He kept in second position for a long time, and after covering 425 miles was in third place behind two European cars. But then a misfortune put him out of the race, the ball bearings on the driving pinion having broken.[1]

When he returned to Europe, rumors of war were already circulating. The disappointing result of the Indianapolis race was soon forgotten in the upheavals of mobilization. Then came the war, and Bugatti's plans for the future had to be shelved.

"In 1913 I had invented my system of reversed quarter-elliptic rear springs," he wrote. "In between winning races, I began to construct my first 16 valve car (4 per cylinder) with a view to entering it for the 1914 French Grand Prix. This was my first car to have my system of low-pressure lubrication and oil feed to rods through oil jets.

"I had great hopes from these innovations, and was eagerly looking forward to the racing season when war broke out. At that time my small factory was employing two hundred people."

CONCERNING "BLACK BESS"

One of the most famous Bugatti vintage cars is the black 5 litre with blue wheels which Roland Garros bought in 1913, and is now known as "Black Bess."[2]

(1) The race was won at 82.47 mph. by Thomas on a Delage of 6,165 cc. Duray on a Peugeot, Guyot on a Delage, and Goux on a Peugeot finished next, in that order.

(2) One of the 1912 type, an open two-seater, 4-cylinder, 5 litre, 100 mm. x 160 mm., a single overhead camshaft, 3-valve arrangement per cylinder. Chassis No. 474. Its full story is told in *The Bugatti Book*, pp. 222-26 (Motor Racing Publications, London), from which these details are taken.

Garros was killed on operations toward the end of the First World War, and it is not known what happened to his Bugatti until it came into the possession of an engineer, Mr. Louis Coatalen, working in England for the Sunbeam firm. A well-known woman racing driver, Miss Ivy Cummings, then acquired it. She had learned to drive at Brooklands at the age of eleven, while her father was at the airfield, and had become a skilled mechanic as well as an expert driver. She began racing in 1919 in a 3 litre 1912 Vauxhall, then in an 11.9 litre Grégoire, a Sunbeam and finally a Bugatti "Brescia"—so was keen on having the "Black Bess." It was she, in fact, who gave the car this name, after her father, Mr. S. G. Cummings, had bought it from Mr. Coatalen. In her hands it had many successes in sprints and hill-climbs, which were a speciality of Miss Cummings, winning at the Bexhill Speed Trials in 1923 and setting up a new record for the Stexton hill-climb at Scarborough and for the Middlesex County hill-climb.

Mr. S. C. H. Davis drove "Black Bess" once or twice, before Miss Cummings sold the car to Mr. L. H. Preston in 1925. He, too, drove it in several races, then sold it to a friend from whom it was bought by Mr. James Justice. In 1935 Colonel Giles acquired the car and had it completely overhauled. It later passed to Mr. R. E. Clarke and, in 1948, to Mr. C. W. P. Hampton, in whose possession it still is and who considers it to be as good as ever.

Colonel Giles wrote to Ettore Bugatti in 1935 to ask about the car's history, and his reply was as follows:

Dear Colonel Giles,

I was very pleased to hear that you have acquired one of my early cars with chain drive. I built only a few cars of this type, which was one of the best models of the period. The first one was built in 1908,[1] and the first sale was in 1912. The car in

---

(1) Very likely an error, as Hugh Conway has pointed out. Bugatti was, in fact, working for Deutz at the time.

your possession was delivered on September 18, 1913, to my friend, the late Roland Garros, the airman of whom you have doubtless heard. This car has therefore an historical interest.

Shortly before Garros was shot down he gave the car to a friend, who ran it for a time and then sold it to Mr. Coatalen of the Sunbeam firm. He was very satisfied with it, and perhaps you could obtain more precise details from him.

There are very few spare parts for this model left, but I should always be happy to make the parts and supply them at cost price. You have only to let me know your requirements. The best thing would be for you to send me the parts needing replacement, as models, thus saving us much searching in back files.

You may be interested to know that the three valve arrangement introduced in this car has been adopted by Rolls Royce for their aeroengines, the patent having expired.

The steering on this car is also very good. I have used it for all my models, from the "Baby" to present-day cars.

The design of the cylinder block, with a part housed in the aluminium jacket, was an innovation for the time. I adopted this design in 1905.

It was, I believe, one of the first cars with multi-valves to be offered to the public. The suspension, with reversed cantilever springs, is another originality.

Yours sincerely,

Ettore Bugatti.

The "Surprising Power" of the Bugatti

An early road test of the 8-valve car was published in the *Automotor Journal (The Auto)* of February 7, 1914:

"What more can a man want of his car in the way of speed than to be able to hold practically any other car that he may meet outside of Brooklands? And if with it he has what the racing car has not—docility and comfort—he would indeed be hard to please if he were not satisfied.

"And these are the qualities that the little 8 hp Bugatti is able to offer him, together with all the refinement in control, steering and suspension that is possessed by the most thoroughbred of modern automobiles—and with the very minimum of charges on his pocket.

"We ourselves had heard much of the capabilities of the Bugatti, and fully expected it to be something above the ordinary, but we confess we were quite unprepared for the extraordinary amount of power with which the talented Italian designer had imbued the engine.

"And whence comes the surprising power? Certainly not from the cylinder dimensions, which are but 65 mm. by 100 mm. bore and stroke, and certainly not from sheer excess of revolutions, for there are many car engines on the market that are capable of turning over at the 2,000 rpm. that constitutes the normal rate of the Bugatti. Rather, we should think, is the source to be found in the valves and valve mechanism, the shape of the combustion chambers and the unrestricted flow of the intake and exhaust gases. But whatever the reason may be, the one fact stands out beyond question that the power is there; and this coupled with the efficient transmission and light total weight gives the car a speed which is comparable only with that usually associated with those of at least three times its nominal power.

"Power and speed, however, are not the only, nor perhaps the most important, attributes of a car intended for use on the road. To find favour with the *cognoscenti*, it must also possess a sense of liveliness, a delicacy in responding to control movement, as ease of gear change, powerful and smooth brakes—in short, it must possess 'refinement.' It is in the possession of this complex quality that the Bugatti ceases to be a light car. Though light in weight and running expenses, no steps whatever have been taken to simplify the design with the aim of keeping down first cost; in fact, it is an automobile of the highest grade, *en miniature*.

"Both the steering and suspension were everything to be desired. In respect to the first of these, we need only say that we have never handled a steering wheel that called for less physical exertion. The rear suspension is somewhat uncommon in form, its peculiar design perhaps accounting for its undoubted excellence."

CHAPTER 7

THE WAR YEARS

As I have already indicated, although my father was Italian by birth and had been living and working for more than ten years in German territory, he was most at home in a French atmosphere. At Molsheim, we spoke French among ourselves; German was the language employed in the workshops. He respected and admired many aspects of the German national character, but was not interested in its culture, being instinctively drawn by nature and upbringing to French civilization.

His decision, in that tragic summer of 1914, was therefore immediate. Others might have hesitated, weighed things in the balance, considered the importance of what was at stake; but not he. The outbreak of war presented him with a choice involving much more than family matters and personal affairs. But as soon as mobilization was declared, on August 2, 1914, he decided to close his factory and leave Molsheim with his family, giving up the rich prospects of his flourishing business.

There was no need for him to have done this. He was greatly respected locally and had many friends in high German circles; people in Molsheim wanted him to stay (his neutral status as an Italian was protected by the Triple Alliance), but he rejected all this well-meant advice. No one ever held it against him, however, so logical and loyal was his line of action.

So we left everything behind. All that my mother was able to take with her in the way of funds to meet living expenses were her own savings, about fifty thousand marks, and a few jewels, in a small canvas bag; for the bank accounts had been frozen. The last train for Stuttgart left at night, and our departure was so hurried that we young children were still wearing nightdresses under our topcoats. The train was packed. We traveled with the Kreisdirektor (head official) of Molsheim, who had been called up; while continuing to advise my father to stay in Molsheim, he took the sleeping Jean on his knees and looked after him until we reached Stuttgart.

The frontiers were already closed, and it seemed that our journey had been in vain. However, my father learned that Count Zeppelin, whom he knew quite well, was in Constance. The Count obtained a safe-conduct for him and his family to cross Lake Constance from Friedrichshafen; and so we reached Italy through Switzerland.

A few months later, Ettore Bugatti wrote to his friend Dr. Espanet as follows:

Milan, 18th November, 1914.

My dear friend,

Your letter of the 6th has reached me. It's impossible to tell you, in my poor French, how delighted I am to have your news.

Luck is of little concern to me, for Italy is quiet and even if she enters this terrible war I should not be called up, and as a volunteer I should not be in much danger. But for you, who are always doing dangerous things, it's even worse just now! You ought to have remained a doctor. May God watch over you!

Our journey was not too bad, as we left Molsheim the day mobilization was declared.

All my horses have gone—you can imagine how sorry I am and how much I miss them.

My dear Espanet, there's more than telesympathy, I look upon you as one of the family.

The Prince Henry Cup car (1909). (*H. G. Conway*)

The first *Pur-Sang* that Bugatti built, while working at the Deutz firm. Four-cylinder overhead camshaft engine, 1,208cc., with semi-elliptic rear springs. Prototype of the famous Type 13. (*Mlle. Bugatti*)

The Baby Peugeot. (*Mlle. Bugatti*)

Friderich at the start, Sarthe Meeting, 1911. The car is a 1.4 litre 8-valve Type 13. (*Bibl. Nat.*)

Molsheim, 1911. The factory was built in the paddock seen in the background after the First World War. The two children in the car are Lidia and Jean Bugatti. (*Mlle. Bugatti*)

Ettore in 1912. He had grown a moustache to look more responsible. (*Mlle. Bugatti*)

The original workshop at Molsheim, 1911-12. (*Mlle. Bugatti*)

Roland Garros at Molsheim in 1912. (*Mlle. Bugatti*)

The 8-valve Type 23. (*Mlle. Bugatti*)

My brother is here in Milan—he saw some terrible things in Antwerp, of course. My father has remained in Pierrefonds; it's a long way off, but we hear from him that he is all right. If you are ever in the district, do go to see him; he lives quite near M. Clément.[1]

Poor old Garros has been reported killed at least a dozen times, then was said definitely to be dead. I'm happy to know he's with you.

Your armored trip must have been awful! I beg of you to write often and give me your news.

Please give my kindest regards to Madame Espanet and tell her that we too should be glad to have family reunions in the New Year, instead of seeing men continuing to blow each other to *confettiture*.[2]

My sister is here with us, and she adds her good wishes to our own.

Your old friend,

Ettore Bugatti.

This letter is reproduced in full because it gives an excellent idea of Ettore Bugatti's detached view of material matters in general. The only thing which seems to have affected him, in all the hurried abandonment of his factory, home and future at Molsheim, was the requisitioning of his horses.

In the meantime, his employees—many of whom were French—had been called up or had gone their separate ways.[3]

(1) An associate of Bayard, an airship constructor, and a great friend of Carlo Bugatti.

(2) Madame Espanet was a Canadian, and never learned to speak French well.

(3) Friderich, whose parents were Alsatians, was of French nationality and had done his military service in France, as previously mentioned. He reached France via Switzerland, joined his regiment, the 8th Artillery, at Lunéville, and took part in the fighting around Nancy and then in the Arras sector. He was awarded the Croix de Guerre in May, 1915, and was then released from the army in order to work with Bugatti on aircraft engines, at the latter's request.

The factory was later taken over by the local authorities. But before then, soon after seeing his family safely to Italy, Bugatti returned to Molsheim for a few days, in September, 1914. He buried the engines of three racing cars in the grounds of his estate, after thoroughly greasing and wrapping them up. These engines, which were of his latest construction, were never detected and he was able to recover them at the end of the war. When he left Molsheim again, he took two racing cars with him by road and succeeded after many difficulties in getting them to Milan. They were stored in a cellar for the duration, but the rain flooded in and damaged them.

While in Italy, he submitted two of his inventions, an incendiary bomb and a quick-firing cannon, to the Minister of War; but the Italian Government showed little interest. In November, 1914, he went to Paris, where he still found many friends and an atmosphere which he had known in his childhood. He stayed at the Grand Hotel in the rue Scribe for many months, then moved into a flat at 20, rue Boissière. Soon after reaching Paris he sought out means of doing useful work, of producing in positive form the ideas which sprang from his inventive mind and were suggested by the pressing needs of the moment. When Italy entered the war on the side of the Allies, in May, 1915, he was "mobilized in France, at the request of the Army Aeronautical Technical Section."

Major Dorand, who was in charge of this Section, at Chalais-Meudon just outside Paris, greeted Bugatti cordially and explained the kind of aeroengine needed. Bugatti set to work at once, alone in his room at the Grand Hotel, to design all the parts of a new type of engine. His designs, which were completed without the help of a drawing office, had no need to be touched up when the engine was being made. Specialists will realize the amount and the complexity of the work involved, as well as the preciseness in visualizing mechanical details.

However, Bugatti had no means of making and testing his engine, a serious problem, especially in wartime. Luckily, his brother Rembrandt was in Paris, having left his studio in Antwerp when the Germans invaded Belgium, and he knew the Comte de Guiche through having sculpted a crucifix for him. Guiche was a Doctor of Science, an energetic young man of wide education who was interested in all the arts. As Duc de Gramont, on the death of his father, he later became a member of the Académie des Sciences and founded the Institut d'Optique. He was intensely interested in all aspects of aviation, but particularly in wind resistance, about which little was then known, and he carried out research in a laboratory at Levallois-Perret, in the northwest of Paris. When he heard of Ettore Bugatti's difficulties, he generously offered him the facilities of the Levallois laboratory to construct his aeroengine. This gesture was the beginning of a friendship and much mutual esteem which became stronger with the years.

Bugatti gladly accepted the offer; and from 1915 onwards, in the laboratory which he turned into a miniature factory, he worked hard on a number of mechanical constructions and inventions chiefly related to aircraft. In particular, he designed and built two aeroengines, one a straight-eight cylinder and the other a 16-cylinder double-bank. This period of his life was probably the most inventive of all, and marked a peak in his career.

In 1917 an American Military Mission led by Colonel R. C. Bolling visited Paris to choose aeroengines for the U.S. Air Force. The Mission was accompanied by a group of civilian experts headed by the aircraft constructor Howard Marmon. Interest was at once shown in the Bugatti designs.

"After visiting several of the Allied countries," wrote Bugatti, "the head of the Mission, Marmon, arranged for my aeroengine to be purchased by the American government. This was the only aeroengine to be produced by the American government under a European licence, and the original schedule was for five thousand engines."[1]

The story is that Bugatti received a nice fat check signed "R. C. Bolling" less than a week after his first contact with the American Mission and, not being used to such promptness on the part of official departments, he went to the bank with the check and ingenuously asked if it were valid.

"As many as you like and for as much as you like, with that signature," was the reply.

All the engine tests were successful. The French government also purchased a licence and arranged for production by Peugeot. This engine was a 16-cylinder double-bank 400 HP design, with a reduction gear and layout enabling a 37 mm. cannon to be fired through the propeller shaft; the whole was covered by patents until 1935. This type of aeroengine was later adapted and produced by Bréguet in France, Napier in England, and Mann in Germany. Many other aeroengines in U-form or H-form are also derived from it.

This aeroengine was the first in France to undergo a successful test run of ten hours, which was followed by another endurance test of *fifty hours* in 1917. "My engines," wrote Bugatti, "showed the successful use of a reduction gear, the only one at that time to have given satisfaction and demonstrated the usefulness of this device."

A tragic accident occurred during the fifty-hour endurance test. An American Air Force sergeant who was watching the test run for Colonel Bolling went too near the whirling propeller and was killed. He was the first American airman to die in active service in the First World War.

A few days later, on December 14, 1917, a "Bugatti Mis-

(1) See letter from Colonel Bolling at end of chapter.

sion" sailed from Bordeaux for the United States, on its way
to Detroit to supervise production of the engine. At its head
were Dr. Espanet and Captain Lepère, an aircraft designer,
and its members included Lionel de Marmier and Ernest
Friderich (who had been assisting Bugatti at the Levallois
works). Espanet and Lepère remained at the Packard factory
in Detroit to collaborate on the building of the aircraft to be
fitted with the Bugatti engine, while Friderich and the others
went to the Duesenberg Motors Corporation of Elizabeth,
New Jersey, where the engines were to be produced.

In the following months, Dr. Espanet flew a Packard aeroplane with the Bugatti engine on many occasions, to the
great satisfaction of the technicians concerned. When the
Armistice came, ten thousand engines were being made, but
the end of the war brought production to a halt.

An account of Bugatti's life during the war years would
not be complete without mention of his friendships. Work
was not everything to him. He opened up when in the company of a few friends, and was more at ease and ready to discuss controversial subjects; usually he revealed little of his
thoughts and said nothing about his projects, although he
was affable by nature. (Outside his family, there were only
two persons whom he ever addressed by the intimate *tu*.)

He was fortunate enough to enjoy several great friendships
during the course of his life—great, because of the value and
variety of his friends, from the highly placed to the humble
assistant. His tact restrained him from ever saying much
about his deep friendship with Duke Ludwig Wilhelm of
Bavaria, the brother of Queen Elisabeth of Belgium. But it
enriched his life, for he and the Duke had equally intelligent
minds and mutual understanding.

Some while before the outbreak of war in 1914 (if I may be
permitted a short digression), the Duke was staying at Molsheim and extended his visit; he was in need of clean linen,

and my father lent him a shirt, the two being of similar build. After the war, the Duke came to stay again at Molsheim; with a smile, he handed my father a small parcel. It contained the shirt lent just before the war.

Two other great friends of my father must be mentioned—Dr. Espanet and Roland Garros, both pioneer airmen and war pilots. They were frequent guests at Molsheim, where their successes in races before the war became family celebrations. Garros won the first Grand Prix of the French Aero-Club, which was flown over a triangular course—Angers-Cholet-Saumur—during a storm on June 17, 1912. But first there were three heats for the thirty competitors. Dr. Espanet was a winner, flying a Nieuport at 80 mph. and at the, then, remarkable height of more than 2,000 feet. Garros was second, finishing 1 hour, 40 minutes behind. All the others failed to finish for various reasons. But the following day the order was reversed, Espanet having run out of fuel when within twenty minutes of the finish.

Roland Garros was the first to fly across the Mediterranean, from St. Raphael to Bizerta in September, 1913, in a Morane monoplane. This exploit was as sensational at the time as Lindbergh's crossing of the Atlantic some years later, and created just as much excitement among the public.[1]

Early in the war, in 1915, Bugatti naturally turned to Garros for advice when studying the means of firing a cannon through the propeller. Bugatti eventually conceived a design making possible the introduction of a cannon mounted within the propeller shaft housing and firing through the

(1) Bugatti wrote to Dr. Espanet from Molsheim on September 26, 1913: "I've received your kind letter. I was both overjoyed and frightened to learn of the pioneer flight that Garros has made, and I hope that he will now take things easy. What worries me is that I keep reading he wants to make a similar flight; this would really be chancing his luck too much. Add your voice, Monsieur Espanet, to my warnings."

center of the propeller hub. Synchronizing the firing of the cannon with the turn of the propeller blades had presented many difficult problems.[1]

Early in 1915, Garros offered Bugatti all the money in his bank account, about two hundred thousand francs—his whole fortune. "You're helping the war effort," he said, "just as I am. I know of your difficulties. You have a wife and three children; I'm a bachelor, and might get killed at the front any day. I wish you would make use of this money."

My father was most touched by this generous gesture and ended by accepting the offer, though he never made use of it.

Garros, alas, had guessed only too well what his fate would be. He dodged it once. On April 18, 1915, he made a forced landing near Courtrai and was taken prisoner, after having set fire to his aircraft and trying to hide from the Germans in a ditch. The news of his capture was a great shock to the French people. Garros was one of their best airmen, and his war record had already increased his popularity. He made two attempts to escape from his POW camp and the third time he succeeded, after twenty-two months as a prisoner. He crossed the frontier into Holland and thence reached France, in February, 1918.

Ettore Bugatti went to see him a few weeks after his return, and noticed some recent photographs of him on a table. Bugatti asked to have one, and Garros wrote on it: "To Ettore Bugatti, the incomparable artist who alone knows how to give life to steel. In admiration and friendship, Roland Garros."

A week later, this noble hero was killed in an air fight. In his memory Bugatti named his second son Roland.

---

(1) A few months earlier a certain Marc Birkham, a Hispano designer, had filed a patent with the identical idea, but Bugatti knew nothing of it.

A LETTER FROM COLONEL BOLLING TO ETTORE BUGATTI

Colonel R. C. Bolling, deputy chief of the Technical Services of the A.E.F. in Paris, wrote the following letter to Ettore Bugatti on September 20, 1917.

My dear Mr. Bugatti,

I have your two letters of the 19th and 20th of September, 1917, enclosing the documents relating to the sale of your 8-cylinder engine to the United States.

Allow me to express my appreciation of your attitude in this matter. I have never known anyone more loyal and frank than you have been in our relations. Moreover, your attitude clearly shows the desire which should dominate everyone's thoughts and actions, that is to say the desire to do everything possible to bring the war to a happy conclusion in the near future. Allow me to compliment you on the path you are following to this end.

I regret the delay in approval from Washington of my recommendations concerning the right to produce your engines in the United States. This delay is no doubt due to the difficulties of conducting affairs at such a great distance. In the meantime, while you sell us the 8-cylinder engine and supply us with all the information which you have given us, I for my part give you, on behalf of my government, the most formal assurances that unless your proposition for the rights to produce your engine is accepted, and until that happens, no use will be made of the engine you have sold us other than as a model sent to the United States to enable our government to test its characteristics and possibilities. In fact, if you wish, and let me know so, I can decide that unless your proposition regarding the rights to produce your engine is accepted, the engine now purchased will be returned to you on request. In that case, however, my government would no doubt expect the purchase price to be refunded.

Very sincerely yours,

B. Bolling, Colonel, S.C.

CHAPTER 8

THE REIGN OF
THE BUGATTIS

Soon after the Armistice, Ettore Buggati took a bold step and made a masterly move. The bold step was to start up his Molsheim factory again; the masterly move was to recover and tune up the engines which he had buried at the outbreak of war. The one and the other, coupled with his energy and enthusiasm and his mechanical genius which was then at its peak, very soon put him in the forefront of the motor world, a place which he then consolidated by a series of brilliant racing successes.

His return to Molsheim was, in a way, something of a gamble. The world as he had known it ten years earlier, when he had first established himself in that corner of German territory, had vanished forever; and no one could tell what the future would bring, whether the new situation would allow similar expansion as had been possible at Molsheim just before the war. When Bugatti saw his factory again, at the end of 1918, it was in such a state that only the walls were of use. What remained of the machinery and tools was scarcely good for scrap. A completely fresh start had to be made, but Bugatti did not hesitate. With his usual self-confidence, he courageously reopened the factory in January, 1919, built some new workshops and restored old ones, and engaged new and reliable workers (a matter he was always most particular about).

To finance his business and obtain some ready money,[1] he sold the licence to produce his engines, as well as a few patents, to various foreign car manufacturers—Diatto in Italy,[2] Crossley in England, Rebag in Germany.

He gathered round him a few of his old and faithful assistants, notably Ernest Friderich, who had returned from America soon after the Armistice; and in March, 1919, the chassis of the 8-valve touring car started coming off the benches at the rate of ten a month. This figure may well seem modest, at a time when the need for mass production was beginning to be felt and firms like Renault and Citroen were planning to produce a hundred cars a day. But Bugatti, true to his standards, took no interest in that aspect of things. As in the past, he was more concerned to create than to produce. And, for the moment, to create meant to pick up the threads of his research and his work where he had been forced to drop them five years previously, at the outbreak of war.

His determination was rewarded by a bit of luck, when he recovered the three engines he had buried at Molsheim and the two cars he had stored in a Milan cellar. He at once set

(1) It should be remembered that Ettore Bugatti built up his business and equipped his experimental workshops by his own unaided efforts. He never received subsidies of any kind, unlike his chief foreign competitors who were given considerable financial help by their governments, notably in Italy and Germany. As for his aeroengines, during the war, they had not brought him a fortune.

(2) The specialist magazine *Motori Aero Cicli e Sports,* published in Turin, carried a long article on the Bugatti 8-cylinder aeroengine in its issue for November, 1916, vaunting the power of the engine, its minimum weight, low fuel consumption, robust mechanism and regularity of action. "This engine which successfully underwent a fifty-hour endurance test is a triumphant addition to the best of Italian machines . . . Let us hope that this instrument of power and victory will multiply rapidly."
The 1.5 litre car was licensed to Diatto in 1919 or 1920.

about putting them into working order again, building new chassis and tuning the engines; and got three racing cars ready in record time—and just as he had conceived them in 1914.

The general arrangement of their engines is worth recalling, for these cars were to dominate racing in the early 1920s. They were an improved version of the famous Type 13 of the immediate pre-war years (4-cylinder, 8-valve, 65 mm. x 100 mm.), with a 16-valve block, originally 66 mm. x 100 mm. (1,368 cc.), then 68 mm. x 100 mm. and finally 69 mm. x 100 mm.[1] The engines had been originally prepared for the light car Grand Prix (usually known as the Coupe de l'Auto) due to be run on August 23, 1914, on the Circuit des Dômes near Clermont-Forrand, in central France. This meeting, of course, did not take place. But six years later, almost to the day, on August 29, 1920, the same engines were used in the cars entered for the light car Grand Prix at Le Mans—the only race organized in France that year.

They had a sensational success. Other starters included a team of Silver Hawks from England, B. S. Marshall in a Mathis, the veteran drivers Guyot and Victor Hémery in a Bignan Sports and a Sizaire-Naudin, respectively, and Violet in a Major of his own make. The three Bugatti drivers were Friderich, Pierre de Vizcaya and Braccoli, a mechanic from Molsheim. The track was in very poor condition, and formed only a part of the present circuit; the rest of the course passed through what had been one of the largest American army camps in France. The appalling state of the course and the difficulties this engendered can easily be imagined.

Friderich shot into the lead at the start, and at the end of the first lap the three Bugattis were running first, second and fourth, third place being held by Violet's Major. It soon

(1) See Appendix I, Types 13, 22, 23. The 66 mm. bore was used in the cars raced at Le Mans (1920), the 68 mm. bore in the "Brescia" (1921) and the 69 mm. in the "Modified Brescia."

became obvious that the Bugattis were not only the fastest but also held the road well and were amazingly easy to handle. A theory generally accepted at the time was that the heavier the weight, the better the car would hold the road at speed. Bugatti, however, thought the opposite; and by the particular arrangement of his chassis proved that he was right.

At half distance Braccoli led the field, with De Vizcaya and Friderich next in order, and with only one and a half minutes between the first and third cars. It seemed reasonable to expect that the remaining laps would see little change. But a race is never won until the finish line is crossed.

With only four laps to go, De Vizcaya called at his pit for oil and petrol, and had a look at the radiator. As he was about to move off again, Ettore Bugatti thought the radiator cap was loose and gave it a turn to tighten it. "Disqualified!" cried a steward. And when De Vizcaya completed the next lap he had the bitter disappointment of being flagged down and disqualified from the race. The decision was badly received by the public, but according to the rules no one but the driver was allowed to touch the car. Bugatti accepted this harsh blow without comment.[1]

He had the great joy, however, to see Friderich win the race with a lead of *nearly twenty minutes,* having averaged 57.6 mph. for the 356 miles. His best lap was covered in 9 min., 43 secs., an average of over 66 mph. Bugatti had made a resounding return to racing after six years of enforced standstill.

The success of the 16-valve cars was even more sensational the following year, in the Italian light car Grand Prix at

(1) This popular story has often been retold, but is, in fact, incorrect. De Vizcaya's mechanic recently revealed (in *Bugantics,* 21, 4) that the car had bearing trouble and a connecting rod had broken. When Bugatti saw this, he walked round and started to unscrew the radiator cap, knowingly disqualifying the car.

Brescia on September 8, 1921. Bugatti had entered several cars in the race; they had an increased bore of 68 mm. giving a capacity of 1,453 cc., roller bearing big ends and a three to one top gear ratio. The drivers were Friderich, De Vizcaya, Braccoli and Marco.

De Vizcaya led on the first lap, with an Italian, Silvani, close behind. Friderich took the lead at quarter distance, but he burst a tire and dropped back behind the Italian. But at half distance he had recovered the lead, followed by the other three Bugattis, and all surged away from the rest of the field. Friderich finished first in 2 h., 59 min., 17 secs., an average of 72 mph., setting up a world record for his light-car class. De Vizcaya was second, only 78 seconds behind, with Braccoli third and Marco fourth; less than nine minutes separated all four Bugatti cars. They had thus swept the board, an unprecedented victory which made the car so famous that the type became known as the "Brescia."

The 4-cylinder cars (with 8 or 16 valves) had opened the reign of the Bugattis in brilliant fashion, but it was the "straight-eight" which enabled Bugatti to dominate racing for the next six or seven years and brought him a string of successes such as no maker before nor, indeed, since has managed to achieve.

For several years, Bugatti had been experimenting with an 8-cylinder engine. In 1913, it will be remembered, he had built an engine of two 4-cylinder blocks in tandem. In 1919, as soon as he had his factory going again, he took up "the problem of eight-cylinder-in-line engines," as he expressed it. The outcome was a 3-litre car (70 mm. x 100 mm. bore and stroke) which caused a sensation at the Paris and London Motor Shows in 1921.[1] However, very few were built; it is not even certain that it got beyond the prototype stage.

Nevertheless, at the end of 1921, Bugatti was designing

(1) Type 28, two speeds, three valves per cylinder.

his Type 30 8-cylinder tourer, and decided to build a few racing cars of this type with a view to the 1922 Grand Prix, which was to be held at Strasbourg in July. They were 2-litre cars with 60 mm. x 88 mm. bore and stroke, but were not supercharged (Bugatti disapproved of this innovation!). They did, however, have hydraulic front brakes of his own design.

They were barely ready in time for the race and little practice in them had been possible. They had mechanical trouble during the race, which was won by the famous Felice Nazzaro in a 6-cylinder Fiat (65 mm. x 100 mm.) at an average of 79.2 mph. for the 499 miles (Grand Prix races were not run over short distances at that time). Pierre de Vizcaya finished second, but was a long way behind, averaging no more than 70 mph. Marco was third in another Bugatti.

The following year, Bugatti sent five of these cars in single-seater form to run at Indianapolis on May 30, 1923. They were driven by Count Zborowski, Pierre de Vizcaya, Prince de Cystria, Alzaga and Rigenti, but all had to retire at one stage or other, except Cystria who finished ninth.

The French Grand Prix was held at Tours that year, and Bugatti had four straight-eight 2-litre cars on the line driven by Friderich, De Vizcaya, Marco and Cystria. These cars were still unblown; they had a short wheelbase of 6 ft., 6 in., but the most remarkable thing about them was their tank-like body. They were probably as ugly as later Bugatti racing cars were to be beautiful. However, they were fast, though not fast enough to win. Favorites for the race were the 8-cylinder Fiats, with the Sunbeam team their chief rivals. But the supercharged Fiats met with misfortune and all had to retire.[1] Segrave won the race in a 6-cylinder Sunbeam (67 mm.

---

(1) Their troubles were due to minor defects and mishaps, but it was the first time that supercharged cars had taken part in a road race, and their lack of success hardened Bugatti's dislike of such a system.

x 94 mm.) at an average of 75.3 mph., with Divo second at 71.8 mph. in a similar car. Friderich drove extremely well to finish third at 70.8 mph., thus separating the Sunbeam team, as K. Lee Guiness's Sunbeam was fourth at 70.5 mph.

It was again the "Brescia" cars that did well that year, winning Bugatti many races of secondary importance. Meanwhile, he was working on an entirely new 8-cylinder car, and the result in 1924 was the most lovely little racers that were to be the hallmark of racing cars for the next decade. This was the famous Type 35, which specialists are unanimous in calling Ettore Bugatti's greatest achievement. Its technical detail was remarkable—roller bearing crankshaft, one-piece hollow front axle, aluminum alloy wheels with detachable rim and integral brake drums—and its long tail and streamlined body made it one of the most esthetically satisfying racing car designs ever produced. Developed and improved over the years, and produced in various versions, this type was for long considered the *Pur-Sang* Bugatti *par excellence.*

Nevertheless, its first appearance in a race, the 1924 French Grand Prix at Lyons, was something of a disaster. Bugatti had given much thought to the race; his usual team of drivers was reinforced by two first-class recruits—Méo Costantini (who drove in his team for the next ten years) and Jean Chassagne (who soon joined him at Molsheim). Bugatti had five cars in the race, all specially chosen; they possessed remarkable acceleration and were probably faster than their rivals, despite the stiff opposition. The Sunbeam team, headed by Segrave, had 6-cylinder supercharged cars; the 8-cylinder Fiats and Alfa Romeos were also supercharged, whereas Bugatti was still refusing to have a blown car.

The trouble, however, came where least expected. Bugatti probably made an error in fitting a new type of tire without sufficient testing. In any case, the team had endless tire trouble, the five cars tearing up their covers and ruining any chance of success, apart from causing great risk to the drivers.[1] Campari won the race in a 12-cylinder Alfa Romeo, followed by two Delages (also unblown cars). Two Bugattis driven by Chassagne and Friderich were respectively seventh and eighth, which was remarkably good considering their tire trouble. But it was still a big disappointment to the Bugatti team.

Success came the following year, when Costantini inaugurated a long series of wins—of which more mention will be made later—with a win in the Targa Florio, the famous Sicilian circuit, and Masetti won the Rome Grand Prix.

The 1925 French Grand Prix consisted of two events. For the 1.5-litre Tourisme, Bugatti modified his 2-litre engine, reducing the bore to 52 mm., and took the first four places. Costantini was the winner, averaging 52.5 mph. for the 590 miles, followed by Pierre de Vizcaya, Foresti and Goux. But in the major event the unblown Bugattis could only finish fourth to eighth (Costantini, Goux, Fernand de Vizcaya, Pierre de Vizcaya and Foresti, in that order). The race was won by Robert Benoist in a 12-cylinder supercharged Delage, after a terrific battle against Antonio Ascari which ended in the latter crashing to his death.

It was much the same story in the Monza Grand Prix. Costantini drove brilliantly but finished third in his unblown 1.5 litre, behind the two 2-litre Alfa Romeos driven by Brilli Peri and Campari, though finishing two minutes ahead of the big, supercharged Duesenberg with Tom Milton at the wheel. Costantini did, however, make the fastest lap, at 99 mph.; while Fernand de Vizcaya, Foresti and Pierre de Vizcaya finished respectively sixth, seventh and eighth.

In short, the Type 35 had given proof of its excellent qualities, but was handicapped by Bugatti's obstinacy in not giving it a blower. When he finally decided to do so, in 1926, wins and records multiplied exceedingly.

(1) See end of chapter for Bugatti's account of the race.

"The creation of my 8-cylinder 2-litre car has been the pivot of all my great successes," Bugatti commented at the time. "I at once put this model into series production, and it is now winning more races than ever, of all kinds and all over Europe, simply and easily in the hands of my customers who thus become masterly drivers. The car has something to do with it perhaps, but as Kipling would say, that's another story . . .

"While perfecting the engine mechanism, much thought had to be given to the car design, for the speed was continually increasing and the horses I put under the bonnet in ever greater number were finding it hard work and were beginning to rebel. The 1923 Grand Prix at Tours saw my curious tank-bodied cars, then there were the handsome lines of my cars for the Lyons Grand Prix the following year, and my famous aluminum alloy wheels. Since then, my efforts have been well rewarded. In 1926 I had telegrams nearly every day, from all parts of the world, informing me of success after success. It was tempting to list them all; they made a splendid total—six hundred by the end of the year.[1]

"All the finest trophies were won easily, by engaging in every important race almost without a pause. . . ."

THE DEFEAT IN THE EUROPEAN GRAND PRIX AT LYONS, 1924

After his defeat in the European Grand Prix, due to tire trouble, Bugatti sent a circular letter to all his agents and customers, explaining in great detail the causes of this setback. The following is a translation of the whole of this long letter:

(1) Bugatti won twelve major Grand Prix in 1926 alone, including: Rome, 1—Maggi; Targa Florio, 1, 2, 3—Constantini, Minoia, Goux; Alsace, 1, 2, 3—Dubonnet, Maggi, De Vizcaya; France (at Miramas), 1, 2—Goux, Costantini; Europe (at San Sebastian), 1—Goux; Spain, 1, 2—Costantini, Goux; Boulogne, 1—Eyston; Italy (at Monza), 1, 2— 'Sabipa,' Costantini; Milan, 1, 2, 3—Costantini, Goux, Farinotti.

Molsheim, 1st September, 1924.

Dear Sir,

Although I have been very distressed by the results of the European Grand Prix, I had decided not to dwell on my defeat and not to draw the attention of my customers to the vicissitudes of this race.

But as I have been constantly asked by friends and customers, and wishing to do justice to those persons who have so loyally shown their confidence in me by letter or in newspaper articles, or who have made other personal gestures, I feel obliged to explain the circumstances of the race as exactly as possible, so that it can be seen that the confidence shown in me could easily have been justified.

First of all, I should like to draw the attention of my friends and customers to a few of the many testimonials which have been lavished on me.

The celebrated car manufacturer, M. Delage, sent me his visiting card with the following message written on it, after himself driving the Bugatti Grand Prix car:

"You have given me much pleasure in allowing me to try out your racing car, and you ask for my opinion of it. In addition to its superb qualities as a racing car, it is the most perfect touring car that any amateur driver could wish for. I am happy to tell you this without any prompting. Cordially yours, Louis Delage."

The well-known English manufacturer of racing car tires, Mr. Rapson, wrote in an article published in the *Autocar* on 1st August, 1924:

"I supplied tires only to the Sunbeams and the Miller of Count Zborowski, although I was warned that in not supplying the Bugattis I was probably missing the winner of the European Grand Prix."

Mr. Rapson wrote to me personally on 15th August. Here is an extract from his letter:

"I was as sorry as you were about the bad luck you had with your tires in the European Grand Prix. Without those mishaps, your car would have won or have finished in the first three.

The tire faults showed the efficiency of your aluminum wheel, which was very satisfactory. I was most impressed by all the improvements you have so judiciously made to your wheel, and I should think that one of the big American manufacturers of car wheels would pay you well for the rights to produce it in that country."

I made a very great effort to enter five cars and to have one in reserve for the first European Grand Prix to be run in France. They were all identical, all with impeccable finish, beautiful body and perfectly tuned. These six cars were ready well before practice began on the circuit.

They arrived at Lyons the day before the first practice runs over the closed circuit. No work on them was necessary, but the drivers washed and polished their cars from sheer pride, to have them in immaculate condition for the start of practice. Everyone was ready at five next morning, and carried out all the tests which had been decided on for that day. No incident occurred during practice, and all the tests were performed without even a bonnet having to be lifted, either at the pits or on the track.

I had set up a camp at Lyons, and those who did not see it will have an idea of it when I say that the equipment was transported in three railway goods waggons and two lorries with trailers. The racing cars went to Lyons under their own power, and the supply vehicles had a load of more than thirty tons.

Everything was provided: the large tent had a wooden floor, there were proper beds for forty-five people, showers, running water in each hut and plenty of electricity. Cooking was done in a well-made hut, and everything was provided to feed the personnel for nearly a month. Ditches were dug on the site to drain away dirty water. Two ice boxes, one very large and the other smaller, were provided. There was also a caravan for my own family.

The tire shape I had adopted after making many tests, first on private roads near my factory and then on the Lyons circuit, had given the best possible results. The composition of the cover and the construction of my special wheel allowed the car to run with a deflated tire; for I had thought it better to risk loss of time due to a flat tire than to carry a spare wheel, which would certainly cause the loss of five minutes on the total time taken for the race.

Everything had therefore been prepared for the best. I was more than satisfied with my drivers, happy with the choice of circuit, and I believed my car to be the most suitable for this race. All the qualities of this *Pur-Sang* should come out on such a track—its rapid starting, good acceleration, more than adequate speed on the straight, progressive and powerful brakes. Everything had been well thought out, was well chosen and ready.

I paraded proudly at the start, driving the reserve car, with my five drivers following in their fine *Pur-Sangs*. The starting flag fell. My No. 7, the car driven by Chassagne, was third at Broken Bridge. When I heard this, I realized that I could be most hopeful about the result, as everyone was supposed to take things easy over the last ten laps.

At the end of the first lap, M. de Vizcaya came into the pits with a flat tire. I had no anxiety; in fact I was happy to see that my specially built wheels met one of the chief conditions imposed in their design, namely to operate without air in the tire.

Everything went all right for a time, but at the end of the third lap M. de Vizcaya came in again with a tread off the tire. There was not a bit of rubber left. The adhesive had gone soft and could be rolled into little balls, thus showing the bad state of vulcanization between the rim and the cover. I then realized that the race was lost so far as I was concerned. M. Chassagne, on the fourth lap, and then two cars together, came in to change rear wheels. I reminded my drivers to be careful, as in tests made previously with other tires the throwing of a tread had endangered the life of the driver. If a tire lost a tread, pieces of it might wrap round the steering-wheel (this had happened to Chassagne) and cause a serious accident. Fortunately, no front tire lost a tread during the Grand Prix, and none of my drivers had any trouble in that respect.

M. Costantini's car, No. 22, had its gear lever damaged by the tread from the right rear tire, and had to complete several laps with the gear lever completely bent and unable to select second or fourth gear, thus damaging the gearbox. So he was obliged to retire from the race. I would point out, however, that his car was driven quite fast over its last lap, proving that no other accident occurred to it, and that it came into the pits and was driven away after the race under its own power.

M. de Vizcaya's car was put out of action through tire trouble. It threw a tread when taking a corner, skidded and knocked down a barrier, then hit the front steps of a house on the first bend into Givors. The car's rear axle was bent and the chassis was twisted, and the driver had to withdraw from the race, to his great distress.

I again told my drivers to take great care, and explained to them the reasons for the two cars being withdrawn from the race. It was due to all these causes that my cars were unable to show what they can really do.

My greatest regrets are not being able to demonstrate the qualities of my new wheel nor show the real speed of my cars.

The features of my new wheel are:

(a) Good cooling of the tire, due to the aluminum rim, which has a greater thermal conductivity than steel;

(b) The cover fixed to the rim by a safety ring enables it to grip in such a way that the cover may be said to become practically solid with the rim;

(c) Perfect cooling of the wheel including the brake drum.

Some people thought that my wheel was the cause of the tire trouble. It is sufficient for me to say that the front tires never budged; so it was not a question of the wheel, nor of heat, but only a lack of adhesive between rim and cover which caused the tread-throwing, probably because the tires were of too recent manufacture.

It was also said that my cars are not fast. That will be seen the next time out, but it is enough to know that when M. Chassagne was informed that he had done a lap only twenty seconds slower than the car which had set up a lap record, he was astonished; if he had known at the time of this small difference he would have made an attempt at the record, for he had never pushed his car to its limits. On a number of occasions my cars passed all their rivals in the winding climb through Givors. This is not to say that my cars were the fastest, for such a statement would not be sporting, but what I can claim is that my cars were the fastest in the climb between Givors and Broken Bridge.

The public in the stands were able to note the following: the continual stops to change tires, the speed with which the wheels were changed, the speed of refueling and the start of the cars with a quarter turn of the handle. Everyone was surprised to see that my cars had no need to be pushed to start them. The mechanic had only to give a single twist and the engine started up, which showed the perfect tuning of the engines and the normal potentiality of these extra-fast cars.

Ten of these cars have been built, and nearly all have been sold. Some are already delivered and are a joy to their owners. They can be used as easily in town as in any race. I hope to make a better showing of the qualities of my product at the next opportunity.

I will end by saying that this car should not be considered a racing car. It has been built on the same principle as all the others, since I do not propose ever to race with a machine that is not strictly the same as is offered to my customers. The engine has only one change, namely roller bearings on the connecting rods and crankshaft, and a special extra-light front axle, round and hollow. All other parts are similar to those of production cars.

The total weight of the car is only 1,450 lb. The high speed is obtained by this minimum weight, by the good shape of the body and, in particular, by the road holding qualities, as speed very often depends on the way the car behaves on the road.

I trust that after having studied the reasons which prevented me from justifying the confidence in my success with these cars, you will feel assured that—although it will not be possible for me to make another effort on this scale—I shall always do my best to enter a race with the maximum chance of demonstrating the excellence of my product to my customers.

Yours very truly,

Ettore Bugatti Automobiles.

CHAPTER **9**

RACES AND DRIVERS

Ettore Bugatti loved motor racing, and there were very few major events during the years between the wars from which his cars were absent. But what he loved about racing was not so much the spectacle nor even the competition. It mattered little to him, in a way, whether he beat this or that rival. But he knew that racing was the one true means of showing the quality of his cars and of enabling him to improve on it. He was also well aware of the publicity he got from racing, and right from the beginning his annual catalogue proudly listed his successes. This was not just propaganda; the results he obtained with his racing cars were, so to speak, within the reach of everyone. All his racing cars were catalogue models available to anyone, and many amateur drivers were only too ready to purchase them. Bugatti was probably the only car manufacturer to market his racing cars alongside his sports models, with both possessing the same features.[1]

(1) His 1927 catalogue, for instance, contained the following racing cars and sports models.

Racing cars:	Type 35—2 litre, unblown 60 mm. x 88 mm.
	Type 35C—2 litre, supercharged 60 mm. x 88 mm.
	Type 39—1.5 litre, supercharged 60 mm. x 66 mm.
	Type 35B—2.3 litre, supercharged 60 mm. x 100 mm.
Sports models:	Type 35A—2 litre, described as "Course Imitation," known at the factory as the "Tecla" model.
	Type 37—1.5 litre, 4-cylinder 69 mm. x 100 mm.

[Continued on p. 75]

This policy was a result of his conception of the role of a car manufacturer, and he once explained this in some detail when commenting on an article published in *L'Auto*.

"If one looks back at car racing, it can be seen that great efforts have always been made; but the work involved is such a hard and thankless task that the car manufacturer, poorly rewarded and aghast at spending so much money on doubtful successes or lack of success altogether, seizes upon the first win that comes his way as a pretext for withdrawing from the struggle.

"M. Desgranges has just given a striking explanation of all this in a prominent article in *L'Auto*. He also revealed another pretext used by car manufacturers—the interests of the customer. It would seem that they have no wish to burden the price of their cars with a hundred francs of racing expenses incurred nor to be distracted by racing, and so they leave those larks to young newcomers.

"The real truth of the matter is quite different—the reason why a car manufacturer does not race is because, even by spending millions, even by employing his best engineers and mechanics, by using his best machines and choosing the best materials, he would not be *sure* of winning.

"He is afraid of diminishing his reputation, and such a car manufacturer will only chance his arm in individual performances which prove nothing and which are given a lot of publicity ballyhoo, or another will only enter events he is certain of winning and which are given publicity with the help of periodicals and papers well paid for doing so. Such car manufacturers will even go so far as to say that the lessons gained from racing are of no benefit to cars sold to customers. And the customer—for whom everything is sacrificed,

[Continued from p. 74]
Sports/Racers: Type 37A—1.5 litre, supercharged 69 mm. x 100 mm.
                Type 43—2.3 litre, supercharged 60 mm. x 100 mm., touring body.

even racing—ends by believing it. Fortunately, car racing has shown that it enables things to be perfected, not the least of them being engines; and everyone has seen how those technical perfections have given us, with improvements in steel and other materials, the engines for aircraft.

"In 1912, 14-litre cars were reaching a maximum speed of 102 mph. in the French Grand Prix; they were the best at the time, but 1.5-litre cars now reach speeds of more than 125 mph. In 1912, cars often broke down, but present-day cars run like clockwork. That's progress, and progress moves on.

"Obviously, it is tempting to stop when you've made some progress, but if you want to follow it up you can't stop. That is why I shall go on, as long as I'm able. I know you can't always win; but when I'm beaten I shall know why, and I'll beat my rival later on.

"There's another thing that ought to be said, while we're at it. When a car manufacturer builds a racing car he always employs the best possible—the best workmen, the best engineers, all the best that his firm can provide. Nothing is too good, nothing is too dear. You've got to win, whatever the cost; you work day and night, if necessary.

"The car built for a customer (the same one as before, of course) cannot be given such attention (which is the best) because it would cost him too much, nor the same steel, because it's too dear, nor this or that, to the point where nothing at all can be used.

"This is a pity for the customer (still the same one). And this is where I would ask you to pay a short visit to my factory, to see for yourself what you would not find in any other car factory in the world—that my racing cars are production models just like my sports cars, and that even my tourers have the same engines and mechanism as my racing cars, are built of the same materials and are assembled by the same workmen.

"You can't tell lies to a thousand workmen, and all my employees will confirm my incredible statement."

Nowadays, car racing is more than ever a matter for professionals, and it is difficult to imagine the enthusiasm and spirit of competition aroused by Bugatti successes. Amateur racing drivers took up the sport for the fun of it and competed against official race-teams in the toughest events. Bugatti was the first to bring amateurs into an official team, though they were all as capable and coolheaded as the best of the professionals.

The enthusiasm for racing cars was enormous, and to enable amateurs with restricted means to enjoy the thrills of motor racing, Bugatti produced a version of the 2-litre model which was only slightly different from the racing car. It sold at a lower price, and was known at Molsheim as the "Course Imitation" or "Tecla" model. It was very popular with sporting drivers, some of whom raced it successfully— sometimes nearly beating the Bugatti Grand Prix car!

Throughout his career, Bugatti always showed a sporting spirit even when competing against the stiffest opposition, and his loyalty to the sport of racing was as much part of his character as it was of his philosophy of life. This showed itself quite early, in the Dieppe Grand Prix of 1912, soon after he had set up in business for himself. His own cars were beaten in the race by Peugeot. The story is told by one of the Peugeot drivers, Jules Goux, who later became famous by winning the Indianapolis Grand Prix.

"It was in 1912, and I was a member of the Peugeot team. We were getting the cars ready for the French Grand Prix (and at that time you had to be able to tune a car as well as drive it).

"The race, which was an important event even then, was to take place over the Dieppe circuit, and after each practice run there were modifications to be carried out on the cars.

A few weeks before the race we engineers and drivers realized there was a bad fault in the engine.

"The 7.6-litre engine turned over at nearly 3,000 rpm., which was 'fast' for the big 4-cylinder engines of the time. The trouble was that the big-end bearings and ball-bearings were of bronze, and the frictional surfaces were bronze and steel (bearings of special anti-friction composition did not come until later). The lubrication process was insufficient for the speed, and the bearings became overheated.

"The remedy was to have crankshafts of more hardened steel; but the firm of Aubert-Duval, which was the most qualified to supply our needs, said it would be at least six weeks before they could deliver. There was not much time before the race, and we seemed to be in a fix. We were all very worried, and tried to think of some quicker way out. Then I remembered that M. Bugatti had a 5.5-litre engine which rotated at much greater speed than 3,000 rpm.

"I set off at once for his Molsheim factory, and was received with his usual kindness. I told him quite frankly the situation we were in, and without a moment's hesitation he revealed a business secret which he could well have kept to himself. 'You've only one chance of solving your problem,' he said. 'That's by having some crankshafts cast in special cementated steel NC.2. To help you get them in the quickest possible time, I'll give you a letter of introduction to the head office of the German firm which can do the job for you. It's in Berlin. I've been using their steel for some time, and I'm sure it will give you complete satisfaction, as it has me. You can go to them with confidence,' he added with a fatherly smile.

"With the agreement of M. Robert Peugeot, I left for Berlin armed with the precious letter and provided with another letter of introduction. Two days later I saw the managing director of the Bismarhutten Steelworks, in Silesia; and just four days after that I left with the four crankshafts we needed.

"And that is how we at Peugeot had a winning racing season in 1912, with no further trouble from the lubrication of the bearings—thanks entirely to the sporting spirit of M. Bugatti, who was one of our most dangerous rivals."[1]

Another instance occurred at the 1922 French Grand Prix, at Strasbourg. This was a most dramatic race, the winner being the Italian champion driver, Felice Nazzaro; it was a tragic race, too, for his nephew was killed while driving in it. Bugatti once again showed his generosity of mind by "helping out" the Ballot team just before the race. Their cars were giving them trouble—the camshaft was vibrating to such an extent that the gearbox worked loose.

Bugatti had cars in the race, too, but a day or two before the start he put some of his men to work late at his factory on making three light camshafts, fairly large in diameter, which were more suitable for the Ballot cars and would enable them to take part in the race with a good chance of winning.

Bugatti's action, like many similar ones of his, speaks for itself.[2]

The truth is that Bugatti, whose self-confidence was equalled only by his impartiality, would have hated owing a racing success to anything but the superiority of his cars. It was an attitude which could lead to his making mistakes, like his obstinate refusal to have supercharged engines, for he regarded a blower as something artificial, almost unwholesome. Not until 1926 did he finally decide to build supercharged engines, and then he produced a model (Type 39, 1.5-litre, 60 mm. x 66 mm., and Type 35C, 2-litre, 60 mm. x 88 mm.) which experts considered as having "an incomparable combination of speed and stability."

It brought him a string of successes, the finest in the eyes

---

(1) From *Cinquante Années de génie méchanique d'Ettore Bugatti*, by Roger Labric. (*La Revue des agents,* 1948.)

(2) *Ibid.*

of sportsmen in general and "Bugattists" in particular being those in the Targa Florio. This race was over the toughest circuit in the world, winding through the mountains of Sicily along steep and precipitous roads; there were twelve hundred bends to each lap, and the race was of five laps—a hellish switchback of 335 miles in all. It was a unique test of the chief qualities of a car—speed, road-holding and robustness—as well as of the driver's stamina and skill.

Bugatti won the Targa Florio five years in succession, from 1925 to 1929, against the best cars and drivers in Europe. In 1925 Costantini was first in 7 h., 32 min., 27 secs., averaging 46.8 mph. In 1926 the Bugatti cars filled the first three places, the drivers being Costantini, Minoia and Jules Goux, in that order.[1] In 1927 the Bugatti winning driver was Emilio Materassi, with Conelli taking second place. Albert Divo, driving a 2.3-litre car, was the winner in 1928 (with Conelli third, Chiron fourth, Madame Juneck fifth and Minoia sixth), and Divo again won this testing race in 1929.

The famous Czech driver, Madame Juneck, was a faithful customer at Molsheim. Although an amateur racing

(1) This great success was shared by the whole population of Molsheim, as can be judged by the congratulatory address made to Ettore Bugatti on September 14, 1926, during his birthday celebrations at the factory (an event which was held every year until 1935):
"The population of Molsheim, represented by the town council and the u/m societies, is happy to express its admiration for the great success due to your undoubted genius, not only in winning the Targa Florio, the Grand Prix of Rome, the Grand Prix of Alsace, the French Grand Prix, the Spanish Grand Prix, the European Grand Prix, the Grand Prix of Boulogne, the Grand Prix of Milan and the Italian Grand Prix, but also the Latin Countries Championship and the World Championship for 1926 (September 5th). September 5, 1926, marks an event which will live forever in the history of the Bugatti *marque*, which you, by your untiring efforts, your great and skilful work, have made renowned and respected the world over. We, the people of Molsheim, are proud to see the name of our town figure alongside your own name at each of your victories."

driver, her experience and skill made her quite the equal of many professionals, whom she competed against in races all over Europe. She was not far behind Divo when she finished fifth in the 1928 Targa Florio.

Méo Costantini was a close friend of Bugatti and all the family. He came of an old Venetian family and was a keen sportsman; for many years he was in charge of the "racing department" at Molsheim—as an amateur driver and without salary—which benefited greatly from his experience and sense of order. There were many occasions for us all to celebrate his successes, gained in masterly style. Besides the Targa Florio, he won the French Grand Prix, the Spanish Grand Prix at San Sebastian, the Italian Grand Prix, and others. He died in 1940, after a painful illness.

The "blue Bugattis" were driven by nearly all the famous racing drivers, professionals and amateurs, during the 1920s and '30s. If their names[1] and their thrilling races[2] are rele-

(1) First mention must be given to Robert Benoist, whose association with the Guv'nor was of the greatest value, through his knowledge of racing and his business ability. For many years he was in charge of the Bugatti agency in Paris, 46 Avenue Montaigne. During the last war he did dangerous work in the Resistance, until arrested in Paris by the Gestapo. He was sent to Buchenwald, and was hanged there on September 12, 1944, at the same time as thirty-five other Allied prisoners.

Williams, an Englishman who won many races for Bugatti before the war and was a very fine racing driver, was also arrested by the Germans. His fate is not known.

Among the drivers in the Bugatti team at one time or other were René Dreyfus, Ernest Friderich, the De Vizcaya brothers, Chassagne, Méo Costantini, Divo, Louis Chiron, Varzi, Nuvolari, Jules Goux and Jean-Pierre Wimille, as well as many amateur drivers all worthy of comparison with the great professionals.

(2) Between 1909 and 1927, Bugatti won 2,136 races:

1909–1914	57 wins.
1920–1924	228 wins.
1925	468 wins.
1926	577 wins.
1927	806 wins.

gated to a footnote, it is because this book is essentially a biography.

The great efforts made by Bugatti to enter his cars in all the great international events, repeatedly marking up a French victory, were given no aid or subsidy of any kind, official or otherwise. After his success on the Eiffel Circuit (Nurburgring) on July 14, 1929,[1] it was reported that the German government had given instructions for a study to be made of the financial aid needed by their car manufacturers to prevent such a thing happening again. The appropriate measures were taken, and the German successes which followed are well known. Similar steps were taken in Italy.

Ettore Bugatti continued his efforts unaided. In 1928 there was a reduction in the number of racing events and he organized an event himself, with the assistance of the Automobile Club de l'Ouest, which was run over the 24-hours circuit at Le Mans. It was for amateurs driving their own Bugatti cars, and the prizes were three of his new models which represented much more than the cash prizes of most of the big official events.

The first Bugatti Grand Prix was won by André Dubonnet, driving an unblown 1.5-litre car at an average of 77.6 mph., with Philippe de Rothschild close behind.[2]

In 1931 Bugatti realized that an answer had to be found to rival cars which were breaking his amazing run of European race successes. His 8-cylinder engine with single overhead camshaft and three valves per cylinder was obviously no longer good enough. Helped and encouraged by his son Jean, who was proving to be an engineering creator, too, Bugatti designed and produced a new model. The significant change in cylinder head layout was the abandonment of

(1) Louis Chiron won in a Type 35C, 2-litre supercharged, aluminum alloy wheels, averaging 66.7 mph. for the 355 miles (25 laps).

(2) See end of chapter for the articles by Charles Faroux on the second "Bugatti Grand Prix" in 1929.

Boulogne Grand Prix, August, 1920. Louis Charavel and his mechanic at the start in a 1.5 litre Type 22 Bugatti (16-valve, B/S 68 x 100, 30 HP). (*Bibl. Nat.*)

Le Mans Grand Prix des Voiturettes. Pierre de Vizcaya at the wheel of a Type 22 (Brescia) Bugatti. (*Bibl. Nat.*)

Lidia Bugatti (now Madame de Boigne) in the grounds at Molsheim. (*Mlle. Bugatti*)

Jean Bugatti in a Type 43 model. An electrically propelled half-scale model had been built for his younger brother, Roland. (*Mlle. Bugatti*)

Bugatti with his two sons, Jean and Roland, on the Lyons Circuit in 1925. (*L'Année Automobile*)

The King of Morocco, Mohamed V, at Molsheim. L'Ebé Bugatti is on the left, and Ettore with Roland on the right. (*H. G. Conway*)

...tore Bugatti on his Irish ...rse "Brouillard." (*Mlle. ...gatti*)

The King of Belgium, Leopold III, at Molsheim with Ettore Bugatti. In the background can be seen the small pavilion where "mirabelle" (plum brandy) was made. (*Mlle. Bugatti*)

A straight-eight Type 30 car, owned by Mr. Peter Hampton. (*H. G. Conway*)

vertical valves and the use of 90-degree inclined valves, two only per cylinder, operated directly by twin overhead camshafts. This was the famous Type 51.

The story has been told elsewhere that Léon Duray exchanged a pair of Miller racing cars (which he had raced at Monza in 1929) for three Bugatti Type 43s. The Miller cars were taken to Molsheim and dismantled, and their engines were found to have twin overhead camshafts and 90-degree inclined valves!

The Type 51 made a good start on its racing career. Williams and Conelli jointly won the 1931 French Grand Prix with it, then Chiron took the Monaco Grand Prix of that year, followed by wins in the Morocco Grand Prix and the Tunis Grand Prix. More successes came with this classic racing car, until the German Auto Union and Mercedes, backed by their government, began to depose Bugatti and Alfa Romeo from their supreme position in motor racing.

However, in 1934 Bugatti and his son Jean produced the 3.3-litre Type 59, of which only six or seven were built. This racing car was based on recent models but had many original features. It had some success in Grand Prix racing in 1934 and 1935, but was eventually outstripped by Mercedes-Benz and Auto Union who were still receiving state support.

In the years just before the war Bugatti won many long-distance races with the 3.3-litre car, and his famous "tank" cars were successful in the French Automobile Club Grand Prix in 1936, and then at Le Mans in '37 and '39. The 1936 French Grand Prix at Montlhéry was won by Wimille and Sommer driving one of the streamlined tank cars. And that winter they won the Twenty-four Hours at Montlhéry with a total of 2,975 miles. "This was in an unblown Type 57S (3,257 cc.), and fuel consumption throughout the race was 13.5 mpg., at an average speed of almost 124 mph."[1]

(1) *Un nom qui devient une légende,* by Roger Labric.

In 1939 Bugatti could note with pride: "My racing cars have built up a unique record, carrying the French colors to victory in competition against teams from all national and foreign firms large and small, and totaling more than ten thousand wins and establishing thirty-seven records which still stand in 1939, a great many being gained at Grand Prix events organized by the Automobile Clubs of the major European countries."

THE "BUGATTI GRAND PRIX" OF 1929

From an historical, as well as a technical, point of view there is much of interest in the two articles which the celebrated motoring correspondent, Charles Faroux, wrote in 1929 about the "Bugatti Grand Prix." They are given below in entirety.

THE PREPARATIONS FOR THE GRAND PRIX

The reasons which led Ettore Bugatti to institute the "Bugatti Grand Prix" last year are well known. The majority of European car manufacturers have ceased to enter racing events, thereby abandoning a powerful means of propaganda just at the time when the American car industry, as closely united as ever, is intensifying its marketing efforts throughout the world and increasing its participation in sporting events. For some time now, Bugatti has been almost alone in carrying the French colors in the international field, and with a success that is well known. The past four weeks have seen, in rapid succession, the now historic crossing of the Sahara by Lieutenant Loiseau in a small 1.5-litre Bugatti, a double victory in the Algiers Grand Prix shortly after a double victory in the Antibes Grand Prix and, to crown all, the win in the Monaco Grand Prix.

We shall pick up again one of these days, certainly; but shall we be ready when that day comes? It is possible to design and build an impeccable racing car, but it is not so easy to train the racing drivers of which the French car industry will then stand in dire need.

Bugatti, as concerned as ever about the general interest, has retained a group of experienced drivers. We already owe to him the emergence of men such as Georges Philippe, Etancelin, Dreyfus, Bonnaire, Lehoux, Lepori, Lamy and many others besides, just as we owed to him champion drivers such as Costantini, Williams, Conelli, etc.

Last year at Le Mans, after the great success of the first Bugatti Grand Prix, the man from Molsheim said "And now for next year!"

And so now we are bidden to be present at the second Bugatti Grand Prix, which will again take place over the Le Mans circuit.

What will the 1929 rules and regulations be?

Last year, the race was a handicap. Dubonnet, it will be remembered, won the final in front of Georges Philippe. This year, Bugatti has adopted a totally different formula and intends giving each competitor the same chance of winning whether his car is a 1.5-litre, a 2- or 2.5-litre, supercharged or not.

Each driver will be allowed the same quantity of fuel. The largest engine may benefit slightly, but the car's heavier chassis should even things up. In the last French Grand Prix did we not see a 1.5-litre car and a car with an engine capacity of more than 3,000 cc. almost finish together?

So all the entries in this year's Bugatti Grand Prix will have the same amount of fuel with which to cover the same distance in the shortest possible time. The rules, which are printed elsewhere, give the amount of fuel to be allocated. Each driver will therefore start with the same potential in motive power, and it is up to each to make the best possible use of it.

This formula is the simplest, and in my opinion the best.

The prizes are the same as last year. The winner will have one of those 2.3-litre supercharged cars which have been the joy of their owners; the second will have one of the new, handsome 3-litre Bugattis, while to the third will go one of the 1.5-litre cars which have so valiantly proved their worth on every kind of track and over all distances.

Let us be grateful to Ettore Bugatti for again serving the interests of the French car industry in such magnificent fashion.

THE GRAND PRIX RESULTS[1]

The race was over 254 miles.

1. Zanelli (2-litre, Dunlop tires), 3 h., 13 min., 45 secs. (average speed—78.5 mph.)
2. Gauthier (2-litre, Dunlop tires), 3 h., 16 min., 36 secs.
3. Sabipa (1.5-litre), 3 h., 19 min., 55 secs.
4. Foc (1.5-litre), 3 h., 24 min., 3 secs.
5. Bouriat (2-litre), 3 h., 42 min., 5 secs.
6. Tetalli (1.5-litre), 3 h., 55 min., 50 secs.

Le Mans, June 2nd (from our special correspondent).

The second Bugatti Grand Prix, due to the farsighted sportsmanship of the Molsheim car manufacturer, attracted a good crowd to the Le Mans circuit. The race was as full of incidents as of vicissitudes, and was won by Zanelli driving a supercharged 2-litre, in front of Gauthier and Sabipa in a supercharged 2-litre and a supercharged 1.5-litre, respectively.

Three cars with blowers thus took the winning positions. However, as I have previously explained, the blower in each case had its pressure reduced and was, in fact, a mixer more than a feed.

Zanelli gave a remarkable display of driving and was in much better form than at Antibes. He bought the car from Philippe the day of the weigh-in, having broken a rod in his own car. Philippe had two other cars in the race; one was a supercharged 2-litre driven by Bouriat, which held the lead for sixty miles, and the other a 3-litre tourer that he drove himself. Both met with bad luck. Bouriat lost time changing plugs, then his hand-pump went to pieces; while Philippe lost most of his oil due to a breakage.

Zanelli had two and a half gallons left in his tank at the

(1) Published in *L'Auto*, June 3, 1929.

finish, which means that his fuel consumption for the 254 miles (at an average of 78.5 mph.) works out at just over 19 mpg. This is a remarkable performance and a wonderful tribute to Bugatti cars and Solex carburetors.

The first observation to be made is that restriction in the amount of fuel to be used is not at all suitable for amateur drivers. They have no means of preparing for such a severe test; and, moreover, nothing fatigues an engine as much as running on a poor mixture. Pistons and plugs all suffer. An incredible number of plugs were needed during the race. The winner, however, never had to stop; and it should be mentioned that he was using Champion plugs.

The quantity of fuel alloted was more than sufficient for the 1.5- and 2-litre cars, from the point of view of the customer. The chief interest of the race was to see how a 3-litre tourer would behave without any special preparation; it was the car driven by Philippe, and had been bought at a showroom only a week previously. It covered several laps at more than 80 mph., and its performance was so conclusive that a number of sportsmen present ordered a similar chassis there and then. My friend S. Singher, president of the Automobile Club de l'Ouest, was one of that number.

There is good news to end with—Bugatti is not only going to repeat this Grand Prix next year but intends to institute a second Grand Prix, also for 1930. I shall have more to say about this later. If all French car manufacturers showed the same spirit as Bugatti, the future of the industry would soon be bright.

Charles Faroux.

CHAPTER **10**

THE MOLSHEIM TOUCH

Visitors to Molsheim came expecting to find a factory, and none was able to hide his astonishment. There was a factory, obviously, and even one of the most perfect of its kind, for Bugatti sometimes found that the machines and tools he needed were not available and so designed and made them himself. His factory not only produced the parts for his cars, but the machines to make those parts, too!

However, Molsheim was much more than that—a house and a family, in the first place, but especially a state of mind, a little world where the attitude to things and the relations between people were out of the ordinary. For me, who had lived there since early childhood and rarely went away, it all seemed quite natural. But for others it was a different matter. The reactions of Garros and Espanet have already been mentioned, and much the same occurred with everyone who visited the place. A customer came to take delivery of a car or to pick up a spare part, and got the impression that he had suddenly discovered, in this small corner of Alsace, the little fief of an Italian *signore* of the Renaissance who had strayed into the industrial age.

Louis Charavel, for instance, told me about his first visit to Molsheim in the early days. He, himself, incidentally, was out of the common run—a young man of good family, who later became a wealthy industrialist, he was madly keen on cars and mechanics, and was not satisfied until he was driving in races. His family, and then his board of directors, opposed his driving racing cars, so he decided to drive under a pseudonym.

"What is it?" he was asked when he went to register at the French Automobile Club.

"Sa bi pa," he said in country dialect, meaning "I don't know." He stepped aside for a moment to have a word with a friend, and when he returned to the desk he found to his surprise that his name had been entered as "Sabipa." It later became famous in the motor-racing world.

Charavel-Sabipa, one of the first people to own a Bugatti, had his rear axle damaged in an accident and came to Molsheim to have it repaired.

"On arriving," he told me, "all I could see at first were some stables, close to a country house. I was only half mistaken. The stables were being used as a workshop, and above them, in the loft, was an office reached by a short ladder. That was where the secretary-accountant, Pracht, worked. I was explaining the purpose of my visit to him when Bugatti came up. He was wearing a colonial helmet and a well-fitting cream silk jacket with a blue border. But it was his shoes I noticed most—to my amazement, they had toes as gloves have fingers.[1] He saw me staring at them, and said with a laugh: 'They're much more comfortable like this. After all, when you want some gloves, you don't go and buy mittens. Why shouldn't it be the same with shoes?'

"Then he took me to see the workshop, where some thirty men were employed. Except for the cylinders, which were made for him somewhere in the Cevennes, everything was produced in his workshop. . . ."

(1) They were actually shoes bought in Germany which had divisions inside the toecap for each toe, and this was shown on the outside by the seams. They could only be worn, of course, with specially-made socks. (Author's note.)

That was in the very early days. But as the business grew, the personality of its founder continued to show in even the smallest details and unexpected ways. "The Molsheim touch" was what the sports writer Maurice Philippe called it, when writing about his visits to the factory.[1]

"What a surprise it is (he wrote), when just outside the typical Alsatian village of Molsheim you come across a hamlet of long, low buildings with brassbound doors of polished oak and with cement paths between them, all so clean and tidy, not a loose stone or spot of dust about anywhere . . . A car factory, that? Surely not! and yet . . .

"It was my first visit to the Bugatti factory. He had asked me to go on a Saturday afternoon—'We'll be able to talk quietly then.'

"There were no workmen about, the place was deserted. And this added to the feeling of being suddenly confronted with something unusual and beyond classification.

"Visiting this domain of the Sleeping Beauty was one surprise after another. I stopped at the door of the first 'workshop' to look at the lock, the catch and the hinges, for all were made of brass and were spotless; nor was there a trace of fingermarks on the copper door-plate. 'Locks made by Bugatti,' the proprietor pointed out. And those words 'made by Bugatti' were to keep echoing in my ears. The explanation of the shining cleanliness of all the doors into the various workshops—I almost wrote 'the various sanctuaries of mechanics'—was quite simple. During working hours, an employee did nothing else but keep the paths and the workshop floors clean—and the door-plates, from which all oily marks left by mechanics were wiped away immediately they were made. Such marks were infrequent, however, for it was a general rule to wipe one's hands before leaving the workshop.

(1) *Souvenirs sur Ettore Bugatti,* by Maurice Philippe; and his article *Les Phares qui se sont éteints* (*Motor,* May, 1958).

"No heed was given to the amount of rags that were used, as I learned later in M. Bugatti's office. He was speaking to M. Pracht, the faithful 'pillar' of the firm, whom it was almost impossible to dissociate from the Bugatti family and factory. 'How many pounds of rags do we use up in a week?'

"M. Pracht told him and then added: 'I've cut down the quantity a little, as there was far too much waste.'

" 'I know,' said M. Bugatti. 'But order as much as before, all the same.'

"M. Pracht's sorrowful look was tinged with admiration as he murmured to me: 'Just can't economize. The workmen know what M. Bugatti is like, and they tell him they haven't enough rags to keep everything as clean as it ought to be. And that's a matter where M. Bugatti always gives way!'

"We went to see the workshops. The machinery was covered with sheets of brown paper. 'It's Saturday, you see. The cleaners come in, and they raise the dust. So the machinery is covered over to keep it off.'

"M. Bugatti lifted a sheet of brown paper here and there to show me some of the precision machines—especially those of Bugatti manufacture. All the vices, for instance, are made here: 'And their jaws are absolutely parallel, whereas in most cases . . .' "

Without going into technical details, it is enough to say that the chassis were almost entirely completed in the workshops at Molsheim. There were the foundries where the cylinder blocks and brake drums were cast, the aluminum wheels and special front axles were made, and the connecting rods cut; while in another workshop the chassis frames were riveted together. Beyond the assembly shops were the test benches with their rows of engines, and the nickel-plating and polishing shops where the work was less noisy but as methodical as elsewhere.

Some aspects of the factory had an even more original character. Bugatti once received a bill for electricity ac-

companied by a letter written in terms which he considered
to be discourteous. He said as much to the manager, adding:
"Come and see me in a year's time. I shall have something
interesting to show you."

A year later, he had built his own generating plant near
the workshops. It was housed in a building as clean and tidy
as the rest, with an immaculate stone floor and tiled walls;
and there was a wheeled platform for carrying out any repairs. "Everything must be kept spotlessly clean," the
Guv'nor used to say. "And with this platform on wheels,
parts can be removed and repaired outside the building."

There was nothing at Molsheim which did not bear the
mark of one man, his tastes and wishes, idiosyncrasies and
even his moods. Everyone called him "the Guv'nor," at the
factory and elsewhere, employees and his family alike. There
were some people who were shocked by this, who professed
to find it vulgar. Yet what better or more natural way of
referring to "Monsieur Bugatti" or of addressing him? For it
always carried respect and trust, with the certainty of knowing that his intelligent and objective advice would never be
refused.

He was always well dressed, and wore his clothes with
quiet elegance whether at the factory or in town. He had a
style and manner all his own. His famous brown bowler was
part of his silhouette; cartoonists and humorist writers soon
noticed that he had pierced some ventilation holes in the
crown, and the consternation this caused among hatters was
a joy to us all. When his bowler was thrust forward over one
eye it meant he was absorbed in thought, was working something out, and no one then approached him unnecessarily.
But when his bowler was sitting on the back of his head
everyone knew he was in a good humor.

The latter was generally the case with him; he was an
optimist on the whole, and had a remarkable gift of observa-

tion which spiced his conversation. He was, then, a man of considerable perception and imagination, genial and generous in every respect, and his egoism only showed if his habits were threatened; but it was rare, for he had a fundamentally good nature, was liberal-minded and impartial. He was excitable at times, young and lively in spirit, tackling problems with enthusiasm. He liked beauty in all things, even in useless, transitory things.

He had a natural creative talent which was the basis of his mechanical experiments, and these were prompted by his artistic sense coupled with a realistic and logical outlook. The cost and the financial return were secondary matters; and to this was due the world reputation of his products for perfect finish and precision.

He made plenty of money, nevertheless, and almost without noticing it. The coffers in the care of M. Pracht, his prudent Alsatian cashier, filled at a rate which would seem bewildering today, though they emptied just as fast. Bugatti used to say that work was never an effort to him, that he built up his business while enjoying himself.

He had little ambition to make a fortune, however. He was not envious of others; like some English squire, his personal interests were in his estate and his horses, and a boat or two. High society held little interest for him, and when obliged to attend social functions he did so without real pleasure.

The truth was that his work constituted his whole life. And in matters of work he had a horror of utopias, of mad schemes. Despite the fanciful nature of some of his inventions and undertakings, he had a sure sense of reality. His insistence on conscientious work, on the job being done properly down to the smallest detail and in any ordinary task, such as shoeing a horse, was evidence of his concern for exactitude; and this made a great impression on all those who lived and worked within his orbit—and on those who still work at Molsheim. A new generation has taken over, but in spite of inevitable changes, the old standards and teachings are still respected. It is not unusual to hear someone say proudly: "The Guv'nor used to say this color was all wrong . . ." or "The Guv'nor didn't like things done that way . . ."

His relations with his employees were personal and cordial, and he was concerned with their well-being both in the factory and outside it. He was all the more aware of their personal problems because the artisanal character of the factory never changed, not even when the number of employees rose to twelve or fifteen hundred.

All of them shared the triumphs and disappointments and took their part in the successful development of a new engine, a new racing car or a railcar (the Guv'nor and Jean Bugatti were the first to make and test a railcar, at their own expense). When Bugatti cars were competing in a race, their fortunes were followed with the keenest interest by every member of this community. The number of times we sat up all night, sending around coffee and sandwiches, all waiting anxiously while some test was in progress . . . listening to the deafening roar of engines, and everyone looking tense and strained, all united by a common hope and concern for the outcome of long experiments . . . That is what remains most memorable and moving.

Ettore Bugatti kept a close eye on the daily work, and sometimes made changes in what a mechanic was doing, according to his own observations there on the spot—to the annoyance of certain foremen. Not that he wished to disregard a necessary chain of command, but he had to apply a new idea the moment it came to him. His brain was always at work; thoughts and ideas which came to him through little details he noticed during the day were jotted down on the backs of envelopes or scraps of paper, and these accumulated in his pockets—miniature archives, yet how important!

(The drawing office would take weeks to translate them into proper designs.)

He had no fixed hours of work. With his natural creative talent he was able to visualize engineering drawings and indicate their essentials with a few strokes of the pencil; simplicity was the essence of his solutions to problems. Such were the characteristics of his methods of working.

He would readily explain that drawing was a sixth sense with him, and was indispensable when studying anything new. It was amazing to see the way he would pick up and feel a car part on his way through the workshops. Holding it in his gloved hands,[1] like a sculptor bringing clay to life or a surgeon feeling for the painful spot, he could tell if there were a flaw and give the remedy, whether in the alloy or the weight.

He had a wonderful visual memory, a photographic mind, not only for things brought to his notice but for imagining creatively in the minutest detail. His inventions and designs varied from an improved form of door-lock and a hinge to the most complicated aeroengines and ships' engines. At one time he became very interested in sailing craft, and produced a roller reefing gear, fishing-reels and the like. Surgical instruments aroused his interest, too, and a friendly firm of precision engineers produced his new trepan. Although he never used a slide-rule, and only rarely a drawingboard, the mathematical figures he gave his engineers always proved to be right. He sometimes spent many hours in the drawing office at night, for he found that the silence helped him to work out problems which had cropped up during the day; but this sometimes led him far from his starting point, to create the most extraordinary things.

His questing mind also turned to religious philosophy,

(1) Gloved because he liked hands to be neat and clean, but especially because the difference in temperature between the bare hand and metal always causes marks to be left on it.

and he used to exchange ideas with eminent theologians and lecturers from the Catholic Institute in Paris, who were often guests at his house. He was also on friendly terms with many leading figures of his generation, and was thus kept informed on a wide range of topics.

This is perhaps the place to introduce the part played by my mother and the great contribution she made to Molsheim. Barbara Mascherpa Bolzoni, as she was before her marriage, belonged to the Milan aristocracy and was the same age as my father. She brought graciousness and gaiety to Molsheim, and her goodness, elegance, beauty and wit were like rays of sunshine to this lonesome corner of Alsace. My father used to say that she was always his greatest support and best counselor; some of those who knew them well believe that "the Guv'nor" would not have had such a brilliant career nor done so much without the help of his wife. In any case, it was her great tact and encouragement which aided him in overcoming, with dignity and courage, the difficult periods with which his life was interspersed.

After the First World War, in particular, when he found the house damaged and pillaged like the factory, her help and support were of the utmost value in restoring and modernizing the family home. Some of her improvements and arrangements were quite novel at the time; for instance, she had a small bar made, with amusing panels by Charles Spindler (a celebrated Alsation artist) inlaid between the shelves, these being filled with glasses of various shapes and bottles of all kinds of drinks. The bar itself was mahogany, and on it stood cocktail-shakers, tankards, and a book of recipes of potent cocktails which were a joy to our guests.

There was a large winter-garden with a tall palm tree and two huge cactus bushes in each corner, and the whole gave a strange impression of contact with the world outside. All the walls were of glass, giving views of trees and the purple heights of the distant Vosges Mountains. In the middle of this winter-garden was a flower bed around a white marble statue about three feet high; this was a work by Rembrandt Bugatti and represented a nude woman seated on a rock. Persian carpets were strewn on the polished mosaic floor all round the flower bed, which was tended throughout the year as though it were in the open. On either side were settees and cane-chairs, almost similar in arrangement, inviting people to sit and talk while sampling drinks from the adjacent bar.

Three fine bronze pieces of sculpture by Rembrandt Bugatti stood against the transparent walls—his celebrated "Antwerp Horse-Fair," "Sick Horses Coming Up from the Mine," and "The Wounded Hind."

The basement had been converted into a cinema, with the seats arranged in small groups and with a few red plush boxes. At the back, next to the projection room, was a glass-fronted compartment for the employees. Films from the Strasbourg cinemas were shown each week—silent films in the early days, and "talkies" later.

This large country house thus became a most pleasant place to stay,[1] and even here the inventiveness of its master was much in evidence. His boldness of execution appeared, for instance, in a large wrought-iron chandelier which he made without any part being soldered—an amazing achievement considering its size and complexity. It was in the dining-room, which he had thought was in need of more lighting (the room was long for its width, had five tall windows at one end and two doors at the other), so he decided to have a double chandelier made by the factory's smiths, who had never done any art-work in their lives. There were seven arms to it, each branching at the end to hold two

(1) During the Second World War it was occupied by the Germans (by the Trippel firm, of which more later), and the basement was made into a reinforced-concrete air-raid shelter with air conditioning, refrigerators and steel doors.

bulbs. In the middle, seven tall lights emerged like pistils from the midst of stylized lilies; and there were four candelabra, each triangular in form and with six branches evenly spaced. The bulbs were set in dummy candles and the shades were of strawberry-colored silk. Ettore Bugatti designed each part himself and supervised the making of them; then, satisfied with the result, he turned from wrought-iron to take up other projects, for he usually had several on hand.

Apart from the production of motor cars and railcars, one could come across a workshop where some leather craftsmen were making or repairing harnesses or suitcases, and another workshop had locksmiths making special locks. Or it could be the special adjustable apparatus, rather like that used in French riding schools, which Bugatti had invented for exercising his dogs, four at a time and according to their age and strength. At one period he had tried to breed wire-haired fox-terriers. The attempt did not last long, fortunately, although he persisted for a few years. The star of the pack was a prize-winner he had brought back from England, Epping Emblem by name. There were as many as sixty dogs at one time, and two men had to be employed to look after them.

However, horses remained his one real passion—apart from cars, of course—and he had fifteen in his stables, all handsome animals. The coach-house contained more than forty fine old horse-carriages of all kinds. The employees would watch the Guv'nor and his horses go past with unconcealed pleasure, like people gazing at something they are proud to own; while customers who had come to take delivery of a car, often from some distant country, were dumbfounded at this unexpected sight.

We lived so much under the sign of the horse, in fact, that when my father decided to have a small hotel, or clubhouse, for visitors to Molsheim it seemed only natural for the name to be the *Hôtellerie du Pur-Sang*. My mother arranged and furnished the place very nicely; there were a diningroom and bar, but only four bedrooms. These soon proved to be barely sufficient, until the time when a typical Bugatti incident enabled an extension to be made. My father suddenly decided to keep chickens and at once, as was his habit, gave orders for some chicken-houses to be built—four of them, an equal distance apart. Then he changed his mind and never bought the chickens. So the huts were converted into extra bedrooms for the *Pur-Sang;* and as each was a small building standing by itself, with insulated walls so that the chickens would not have been either too warm or too cold, many guests preferred these bedrooms to those in the main building.

CHAPTER **11**

SECRETS OF
THE "PUR-SANG"

"Ettore Bugatti—mad inventor or mechanical genius?" was
a question put by Hugh Conway in one of his articles. He
then went on to answer it himself:

"Viewed from the point of view of his car designs and
productions, he was certainly a mechanical genius although
few engineers would doubt that he had a streak of ec-
centricity or stubbornness which made him persist with bad
design features long after their faults had become obvious
to his customers. But viewed after a study of his inventions it
is not so easy to form an opinion. Many of his patents are
unbelievably odd, and impracticable, examined thirty years
after they were filed. Considered in total and attempting to
put them in perspective, they are fascinating."[1]

It is not the purpose here to enter into technical contro-
versies; they can be left to far better qualified specialists to
pursue. But it may be worth while to take a closer look at
this important aspect of Bugatti, in order to reach a better
understanding of the man. He was not a qualified engineer;
he had received no technical education and possessed no
diplomas. He had learned as he went along, from experience

(1) *Trans. Newcomen Society*, 31, 1959. "The Automotive Inventions
of Ettore Bugatti," by H. G. Conway.

which increased with the years, and a natural mechanical ability aided by a gift of observation had soon made up for these deficiencies, though in some rather odd ways during his early years.

For instance, when he was only eighteen and working for Stucchi, he noticed a Soncin engine which was cooled by copper blades. "I didn't know what the thing was," said Ettore, telling the story many years later. "I thought it was electricity! But when I'd dismantled it all, I said to myself 'What a mess it is! I must put this right.' I told Stucchi what I thought of doing. He was very interested and said 'It's a good idea.' And that's how I began to understand internal combustion engines."

This same intuition soon led him to adopt solutions of his own which were, it would seem, remarkably effective. Louis Charavel, who purchased one of the first cars produced at Molsheim, had this to say of it:

"I was struck by the simplicity and directness of the mechanical solutions. Bugatti had introduced a banana-shaped tappet between the cams and the valves, and the camshaft actuated the curved tappets. But in particular, by acting contrary to what was generally taught, he had grasped a factor which was misunderstood at that time. In technical schools, apprentices were taught that outlet valves had to be wider than inlet valves because the volume of gas was greater. Bugatti was the first to do just the opposite, making his inlet valves the larger—which is what everyone does now . . ."

Bugatti's natural mechanical ability was enriched by practical experience and enabled him not only to produce his famous models such as the "35," the "43" and the "57"—to mention the best known and most successful—but also to develop a feeling for engines and their mechanism, a flair or kind of instinct which at times seemed to border on the miraculous.

An example of this occurred at the Monza Grand Prix in 1926, in which the Bugatti cars were to be driven by Charavel (Sabipa) and Costantini. Bugatti had entered his 2.3-litre cars, and when he heard that Segrave would be driving a 6- or 7-litre Napier he said to Charavel when they were having lunch together the day before the race: "You know Segrave quite well. Do you think he would let me see his car?"

Charavel put the question to the crack English driver, who said with a smile: "He wants to have a look at the car that is going to beat him, does he? Well, why not—he can't do anything by just looking at it."

So Bugatti went to the garage, walked round the car and gazed at the mechanism for a few minutes. Then he turned to Segrave and said: "You won't finish the course on Sunday, you know."

"Are you trying to discourage me?" Segrave retorted.

"Before the half distance, your engine bearer will break," Bugatti calmly continued. "And that will be lucky for you, as your front axle seems to be unsafe, too."

Segrave thanked him coldly, and later said to Charavel: "He's trying to put me off, but he'll see! On Sunday I'll put a few laps between my car and his!"

On the Sunday, before the start of the race, Bugatti advised his own drivers to keep their distance from Segrave. And it was fortunate that they did so, for at half distance the crankcase arm in question broke and Segrave had to retire.

During the race—which was won by Charavel—Bugatti also gave proof of his intimate knowledge of his own cars. While lapping at about 110 mph. early in the race, Charavel lost the tread of his left rear tire, which then burst. The car carried no spare; Bugatti had said "You can get back to the pits at 110 mph., the cover won't leave the rim and the car will hold the track." And indeed it did, at 100 to 105 mph. It bumped now and again, but the centrifugal force prevented it from running on the rim. Charavel changed the wheel and set off again . . . only to burst a tire, again the left rear and at exactly the same point, on the Esure bend. When he returned to the pits, Bugatti said to him this time: "Take just a second less, a second and a half less, going round the Esure—and you won't tear up the tire."

The Esure hairpin, the sharpest of all and a right-hand bend, was always taken with maximum contact. Charavel was a little surprised by Bugatti's advice, but reduced speed by six or seven miles as he took the bend—and the rear tire held. Between laps, Bugatti had puzzled over the cause of the accident, imagining the car taking the bend, and had realized that it was due to the traction being too great.

He was so much a part of his cars that one would almost have said at times that he was lapping the course in their place, experiencing the frictions and all the stresses and strains imposed on the chassis and engine.

It was just the same when a model was in an early stage of production or still on the drawingboard, as his assistants often had cause to know. For instance, he and Costantini were in the drawing office one day, examining a design drawn up by Kortz, a very good engineer trained at the Zurich Polytechnikum.

"There are two faults in it," Bugatti said after a minute or two, and without making a mathematical calculation. "The rear axle is not strong enough; and the cardan-shaft forward of the gearbox is too big, and can be reduced in size."

"The rear axle can be made stronger, if you wish," Kortz agreed on reflection. "But it's impossible to reduce the cardan-shaft; it would get twisted."

"All right, we'll have two models made," retorted Bugatti, "one with your measurements and the other with mine."

This was done, and the two chassis were put on test. The

cardan-shaft made to Bugatti's measurements stood up well, but the smaller one designed by Kortz failed.

One had only to see Bugatti handling a car part, as mentioned earlier, to realize what it conveyed to him. And so he went on improving and perfecting his engines and cars, fingering pieces of machinery just as he felt a horse's legs after a ride or when he made his daily visit to the stables. He treated machines as he did his horses, unwittingly perhaps, lavishing care on them in order to obtain the best results.

He was in a most angry mood one day because he had discovered a hammer in the assembly shop. He had the culprit brought to him, and gave the man the rough edge of his tongue. His wrath was long remembered, and it had good effect. He believed that parts which had been properly measured and well turned on the lathe should fit easily enough, and that they were spoiled by being knocked into place with a hammer.

This minute attention to detail is probably the reason for the almost musical sound of a Bugatti engine, even when at its loudest.

Bugatti's curiosity about mechanical things was always fully alert, even about quite ordinary objects and contraptions, which explains the extraordinary diversity of his numerous patents. Their total is thought to have reached 941, filed chiefly in the U.S.A., Britain, Germany and Switzerland.

He patented the name *Pur-Sang*[1] on June 19, 1911, and a little later he filed his bevel-driven overhead camshaft. His famous arrangement of a cross tube to which was at-

---

(1) Contrary to general belief, the shape of the Bugatti radiator was not adopted from that of the horseshoe. Young Bugatti was influenced by the oval shapes of the furniture designed by his father, and based the form of his early bonnets and radiators on them. He later modified the shape of the radiator according to changes made in the construction of the engine (see sketches).

tached the special reversed fixed cantilever springs forming the rear suspension was patented in France, Britain, Germany, the U.S.A. and even Russia between 1911 and 1913.

In 1911 he devised a system of bandagings and hoops to replace tires, and his patents previous to 1914 included ultralight frames for bicycles and motorcycles, an elastic rubber handlebar (to eliminate vibrations) and a bicycle saddle, while he was also working on tip-up seats for motor cars.

One of his more interesting patents was his hydraulic brake which he invented in 1918 and put into the models he exhibited at the 1920 Paris Motor Show. A number of these brakes were made entirely at the Molsheim factory and were used in several cars sold to customers and in the "tank-

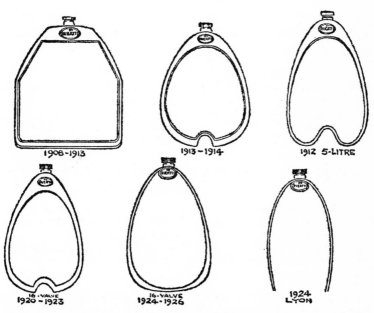

The changing shape of the Buggati radiator between 1908 and 1924, from the square "Mercedes" type to the peardrop of the 16-valve and the horseshoe of the Type 35. The development, as can be seen, was purely esthetic. (Drawings by Bob Shepherd)

bodied" racing cars for the 1923 French Grand Prix at Tours. A special fluid and leather tubing were required for these hydraulically operated brakes, and Bugatti was unable to find a firm interested in manufacturing them. His patent expired, and his idea was later taken up and used in the well-known Lockheed brakes, which had features similar to those of the brakes that Bugatti had shown in 1920.

He invented a number of machine tools, from an apparatus for fitting gudgeon pins (patented in France in 1918 and in the U.S.A. in 1923) to a turning lathe (1925) and a laminating machine. He concentrated, however, on making precision tools for use in his own factory, and thus patented a number of milling machines, turret lathes, slide lathes, cutting machines, beveling tools and drills.[1] His one thought

---

(1) It would be tedious to enumerate all the Bugatti patents which had no particular connection with road vehicles, and some of which were rather eccentric.

In 1916 he devised a mechanical razor on a tubular support and a chain-snap for snares, which he patented in France and Germany. In 1911 his inventions had included a special kind of screw, car springs, a direct gear-change, and a water pump connected with the cooling system. Later, he invented a trepan and several other surgical instruments. In 1910 he had produced one of the earliest "honeycomb" type of car radiators.

He experimented with a tire having a double innertube in 1923–24, and also with a safety device to fix tires to the rims. In 1924 he patented his system for four-wheel brakes and invented his disc wheel.

In 1936–37, while engaged on major projects (a new type of bogie wheel for his fast railcars, and the engines for them—his aim was to have a "rail-holding" quality comparable to the "road-holding" of his cars) he turned his mind to aircraft design and patented several improvements to propellers and a rudder of his invention.

A somewhat unexpected invention of his should not be omitted—a fishing reel for catching tunny and other large fish, which he intended to try out if he ever had the time to go cruising in his yacht off the coast of Sicily.

In 1939 he filed a specification for a boat's engine with reverse gear, and another for a torpedo-boat. In 1942 he designed a lightweight Moped and tested the prototype himself.

was to have the perfect tools for a product whose finish and quality would be unequaled anywhere in the world.

All this individuality of everything manufactured at Molsheim sometimes had its inconveniences. There was the time, for instance, when Bugatti invented some special bolts and wing-nuts which seemed to him more sensible and practical to use, but which could not, of course, be obtained anywhere else.

Nevertheless, in such circumstances he maintained an obstinate belief in his own engineering skill, and this refusal to meet objections naturally resulted in his making some mistakes, such as not using a blower until several years after other car manufacturers. However, he had the sense to give way and accept facts in the end. But there were times when he liked to be high-handed.

A story is told that a customer once complained about the poor brakes on one of his models, and he merely replied in lordly fashion: "My cars are made to travel fast, not to stop!"

The Bugatti "Caravan"

In Bugatti's own account of his misfortunes in the European Grand Prix at Lyons in 1924, there was mention of a caravan for his family. It was not exactly an invention, but a description of it would not be out of place here. He fitted it out with a number of gadgets and enjoyed making it a most luxurious and modern vehicle for that time.

I have only a hazy memory of what started him on it, but once the idea began to take shape, I remember we were all enthusiastic and excited by the prospect of adventurous journeys. My father's fertile mind got to work on building a "caravan" which could be coupled to a truck, drawn at speed along the main roads, and taken up the most twisting mountain roads.

When completed, it was a little masterpiece of road transport, and was made entirely at our Molsheim factory. Its size was the maximum then permitted on the roads (in 1924), the length being quite seventeen feet and the width that of an average truck. Inside, the height of the roof was similar to that of the ceiling in a good-sized bedroom. Mounted on a four-wheel chassis and with excellent suspension, it had all the stability and flexibility resulting from the best techniques of car construction.

The sides and roof were made of the very best oak, with a metal framework, so the whole was sturdy yet light, and warm to the eye. Two small windows (14 in. x 12 in.) were in the front. This wall had a large wooden panel with inlaid work representing a flight of storks, another piece of marquetry by Charles Spindler. The sides had three windows at shoulder height, each with a wooden shutter and metal screen which could be slid down, like the window itself, from inside. These side walls were covered with more marquetry work by Spindler, representing scenes of Alsatian village life and the countryside.

A generating machine provided good lighting, and there was even running water available! A tank holding a ton of it was installed on the roof, which was also fitted with ventilators.

The exterior was painted with white lacquer. A short flight of steps at the back (which could be pulled up or let down like the steps of an old-fashioned coach) gave access through a fine oak door with polished brasswork, like the doors at the factory. Under the floor were large drawers which were opened from outside. To the right of the entrance was the kitchen, lighted by a big window and equipped with a solid-fuel cooker, a sink and—discreetly hidden—a garbage pail. Adjoining the kitchen was the toilet, which also had its water supply.

The main part was turned into a diningroom when we had a shooting party. It had space for sixteen to eighteen people to sit to table; three at the "high table" and the rest along the sides, on comfortable leather benches, at two long, narrow tables. The space in the middle was thus left free for the servants to serve the meal. When the tables were laid they made a most comforting sight for the sportsmen returning cold and famished.

The truck had a platform at the back, with a hood, and this served as a "second-class diningroom," as it was called. There, the beaters and the youngest of the guns ate together in high spirits, although somewhat cramped for space. Wood fires crackled round the vehicles, warming the atmosphere. The meal ended with glasses of *mirabelle* (plum brandy) made by my father in his own little distillery from fruit gathered on the trees (not bruised from falling), which left us all in a state of euphoria.

My father was not really keen on going shooting, neither was Jean; but they both liked the friendly atmosphere and the party occasions. My father would follow the others on horseback, but kept some distance from them. The shoot was over a wide plain extending northward from the factory to the Altdorf woods, a small but lovely forest about twelve miles from Molsheim in the direction of Strasbourg.

There was plenty of game. One of the factory engineers, a friend of the family and a keen sportsman, saw to it that good shooting was to be had; he was in charge of the covers throughout the year, and also took on the difficult task of training the dogs. Augustin Walter was an elegant figure in his chestnut overcoat and always had a courteous smile; he is still sadly missed by all the family.

During the last war the "caravan" was taken away by Trippel, Himmler's friend, who had seized all our property; and it was discovered after the war, half demolished, in the forbidding internment camp at Struthof, some thirty miles from Molsheim.

Charles Spindler died a few years before the war, so never knew of the destruction of the panels on which he had worked with such zeal. His death was a loss to every Alsatian. My mother sent a wreath of white carnations, red roses and blue cornflowers, arranged in one of those large Alsatian black silk headdresses that form part of the women's regional costume, with a narrow red band to represent the Legion of Honor which had been awarded to him a short time before his death.

His son Paul has continued in the craft, and still executes fine marquetry work in the village where Charles Spindler was born, Saint Léonard, near Obernai.

CHAPTER 12

"SIXTY MILES AN HOUR ACROSS THE SAHARA"

An account of Ettore Bugatti's career during the 1920s, when his racing cars reigned supreme, would not be complete without some mention of the exploit of Lieutenant Frédéric Loiseau, who drove across the Sahara and back—nearly ten thousand miles—in a 1.5-litre Bugatti tourer. Such an exploit was, of course, a great sporting achievement; but it also confirmed what Bugatti had always maintained: that his cars were not monsters made only for racing, but vehicles which, in the hands of any capable amateur driver, would give proof of their exceptional qualities.

Lieutenant Loiseau first had the idea of this expedition in 1927. It was then his intention to cross the Sahara to Lake Chad in ordinary touring cars.[1] He put the idea to the French Resident General in Tunis, Lucien Saint, and succeeded in obtaining his support. Loiseau then approached Bugatti to ask if he would care to supply the vehicles for the expedition. Bugatti examined the whole proposition and found it to be a bit risky but feasible; and as he was always prepared to give his backing to undertakings of this nature, he agreed to Loiseau's request.

(1) Lt. Loiseau published his account of the expedition in his book *A 100 à l'heure à travers le Sahara* (La Diffusion du Livre, Algiers), from which the following extracts are taken.

Bugatti's contribution to the expedition was formally set out in the following letter:

Molsheim, 23rd January, 1928.

In view of the agreement made in Tunis on 17th December, 1927, between M. Lucien Saint, French Resident General for Tunisia, and Lieutenant Frédéric Loiseau, leader of a proposed crossing of the Saraha to Lake Chad in touring cars of series production:

It is hereby agreed that M. Ettore Bugatti, car manufacturer at Molsheim, will give the following aid to Lt. Loiseau and his associates, as evidence of his sporting interest in the success of the expedition.

M. Bugatti will build for the expedition a series of five or six chassis of the 4-cylinder 1.5-litre type, with all the bodywork and equipment necessary for a crossing of the Sahara, to be delivered within three months of being ordered, such order to be given in no more than three months from the above date.

M. Bugatti undertakes to supply to Lt. Loiseau and his associates for *the duration of the expedition* (about 5,000 miles in two and a half months):

(a) All tools and spare parts needed,

(b) All the Dunlop tires necessary between the starting point in North Africa and the return to France.

In addition, he will lend the expedition one of the mechanics from his factory.

(signed)   Ettore Bugatti.

"That was the beginning of it," Bugatti later noted on the copy of this letter of agreement. "But instead of crossing to Lake Chad, it was the Ivory Coast and those distant parts —twice the mileage but in half the time."

Lt. Loiseau gave a lighthearted account of his visit to Molsheim, one day in 1928, to take delivery of the vehicles:

They were lined up under a hangar. I noticed at once the intelligent thought that had been given to certain details in view of the use to be made of the cars. They were 1.5-litre chassis (10 HP) and had been given an extra fuel tank made of light metal to hold about fifty gallons. The front seat had a running board with a battery on either side; and there was an oil-suction hand-pump, as in racing cars, with a reserve supply of four and a half gallons under the seat. The engine was geared up slightly less than usual, and the water circulation system was very simple. There were no wings; I had the wind-screen and cowling taken off the car I was going to drive, and this gave me total visibility.

Ettore was gazing at the five "saharians" like a horse-breeder at particularly fine thoroughbred foals. Just then, there was a sound like gunfire, and Jean (Bugatti) came dashing up in his usual way on his powerful motorcycle, tearing up a bit of asphalt and a lot of his tires, as he braked sharply and stopped a few inches from the obstacle and from us.

Ettore said: "Monsieur Loiseau, I guarantee my cars for ten thousand miles away from roads. Of course, they mustn't hit potholes of more than a yard. But a yard is all right!"

Myself: "I'll see I don't risk more than half a yard, M. Bugatti."

Ettore: "Yes, but you're the only one to believe in this attempt! The others are only doing it to get their names in the papers. In an expedition like this, one man must be in command. Will you be able to get these others to obey you? I'd be very upset if these fine cars were handled care-lessly . . ."

Jean: "But, father, Lt. Loiseau is used to giving orders. It's his job!"

Ettore: "To soldiers, yes. But with civilians it's more difficult."

Myself: "What matters, M. Bugatti, is to get started. After that, they'll have to follow me or die of thirst!"

Ettore: "Be very adaptable and don't take chances, M. Loiseau! Incidentally, I'm not giving you any spare parts be-yond the usual bits and pieces. In the first place, you wouldn't know how to use them; and then, it's impossible to tell what might break on a journey of this kind. You'd have to take a whole car in spare parts . . ."

Jean: "Don't bother the lieutenant, father! He'll make a success of it, I'm sure. You don't know anything about the Sahara!"

Jean was right. Lt. Loiseau did make a success of it, although not without a number of mishaps, as was only to be expected—and which showed what Ettore Bugatti had meant. There was, for instance, the "fine bit of straight" where Lt. Loiseau stepped on the gas:

"Now mind how you go," said Labouret (Loiseau's companion, who had joined him after the start).

Sixty, sixty-five, seventy . . .

"Look out!"

It was too late. There was a huge gap of at least five feet right across the track. For a moment, it looked like the end of our journey.

Clinging to the wheel, I had kept my foot right down on the accelerator and had not touched the brake, in what was probably the one decisive reflex action of the whole adventure. The car took off from the ground like a thoroughbred jumping a stream and landed on all four wheels without stumbling, in the best style, but with a creaking, shuddering protest from all the steel and aluminum. I braked.

A few seconds later we were out of the car, very shaken but laughing to find ourselves unhurt, and examining everything. Nothing had budged, neither the chassis, nor the steering, nor the back axle. Only a jumble of tools, mess tins and bananas had been tossed about. Bravo, Bugatti! and long live Dunlop! And many thinks, Repusseau, I exclaimed with a surge of gratitude . . . for if a tire had burst or the steering had given way . . . or if the shock absorbers had not been so excellent! . . .

"And when I think," said Labouret, "that we'd have spent

Friderich at the wheel of the Type 22 which won the Grand Prix des Voiturettes in 1920. (*Bibl. Nat.*)

The Bugatti "Tank Cars" at the Grand Prix, Tours, 1923. Left to right: Vizcaya, Friderich, Prince Cystria, Pierre Marco, at the wheel. (*H. G. Conway*)

Lyons, 1924. The Type 35, one of Bugatti's most famous racing cars. (*H. G. Conway*)

André Dubonnet, after winning the Bugatti Grand Prix at Le Mans, 1928. (*A. Dubonnet*)

San Sebastian Grand Prix, 1924. Left to right: Pierre de Vizcaya, Costantini, Chassagne, Soderini. (*L'Année Automobile*)

Ettore Bugatti at Lyons, 1924. (*L'Année Automobile*)

Bugatti wearing the driving helmet he made by cutting off the rim of one of his bowler hats. (*L'Année Automobile*)

Louis Chiron in a Bugatti winning the Monaco Grand Prix, 1931. (*Louis Chiron*)

Two Type 54 Bugattis at Brooklands (Kaye Don driving the leading car). (*Motor Racing Publications*)

hours trying to get around if we had seen in time that the bridge was missing."

"To drive from Gao to Niamey in nine hours (wrote Loiseau, after his brilliant and successful exploit), meant covering three hundred miles at a good average speed. It also meant that the Sudanese town, the nearest to French North Africa, was brought within reach of the capital of the Niger in an undeniably practical manner. To travel from Ouagadougou to Grand Bassam in two days meant clocking up eight hundred miles at a rate never before known down there, and more than anything that the capital of the Upper Volta, a region without railways and far from the sea, had been brought within reach of an Atlantic port.

"To drive from the capital of the French Sudan, Bamako, to Timbuktu and Gao, the head of the Trans-Sahara route, a thousand miles across difficult desert sands with few real roads and good tracks, is undoubtedly a sporting record and only a Bugatti has been capable of it so far. For the colonial officer or administrator returning home to France from Gao, and who has to take the train at Bamako, it means that his traveling time is cut by six weeks.

"There is also the fact that letters were carried from Timbuktu to Algiers in six days, whereas they sometimes take more than two months. The journey from the Niger to southern Algeria, across the Sahara, was done in forty-two hours, which included a nine-hour stop.

"The conclusions to be drawn from all that are obvious. If a private person can drive nearly ten thousand miles through French African territory in a month, without any special knowledge of the desert regions or of car mechanics, and making average speeds which would often seem very good on the fine roads in France, what could not be attained by an official, properly organized expedition?"

Lucien Saint wrote to congratulate him in the warmest terms:

28th September, 1929.

My dear Loiseau,

You ask me for a few lines on your expedition across French Africa; and you modestly tell me that you only carried out a round tourist trip, for you set off—alone, as it turned out—in a standard car with a van body and carrying no spare parts. In this way, you wished to prove that nothing was impossible and that the Gulf of Guinea is only a matter of hours from Oran by an overland route.

In thirty-two days you made a dashing return journey, covering ten thousand miles and setting up a record crossing of the Sahara on the return trip, when you covered the thousand miles of desert between Gao and Adrar in thirty hours, from one a.m. on 1st March to seven p.m. on the 2nd.

You set up other records in African communications. In six hours you linked Gao, the terminus of trans-Sahara routes, with Niamey, the capital of the Niger; and in two days you made the journey Bamako-Timbuktu-Gao, crossing many different regions, from desert sands to tropical forest, as we should drive from one county to another.

In this way, we are showing that we are no longer satisfied with coastal journeys around the immense land of Africa, unknown and mysterious until quite recently, but are striking inland and pioneering routes for that means of travel of the future, the motor car, which enables individual journeys to be made and responds to each person's whim.

You have proved that the most inaccessible parts of Africa are open to factory-produced, standard cars, to the tourist and traveler alike; you have pushed back the frontiers of the mysterious and transformed geography to man's will.

Bringing different regions nearer to each other by motor car is a new conquest of our epoch, and you have made a contribution to a century avid for knowledge and never satisfied, making it possible for everyone—if they have your pluck—

to journey from the familiar shores of the Mediterranean to the mirages of the Sudan.

And so the motor car is of the nature of the ancient gods of Olympus, being a new centaur adaptable to new climes, and lord of time and space.

With my warmest congratulations on your fine exploit,

Yours sincerely,

Lucien Saint.

French Resident General in Morocco.

Bugatti wrote two days later:

Molsheim, 30th September, 1929.

My dear Loiseau,

I must admit that I did not think your expedition would be successful.

First, because an expedition calls for long preparation, for nothing being left to chance and all possible eventualities being foreseen. Second, however sure one is of the good quality of one's product, of the reliability of the material and the fearlessness of the driver, there is always the possibility of the unexpected when traveling ten thousand miles over sand dunes and along rocky tracks.

Nevertheless, you were successful.

This exploit is most informative and throws light on a number of problems. In particular, it shows that very fast communications are possible between Algeria and the various Colonies, and by ordinary motor vehicles.

I am more interested in this success than in any other, for to have driven ten thousand miles in such conditions, without the slightest mechanical trouble, is a truly remarkable feat.

I am not forgetting, however, that the greatest merit is yours, my dear Loiseau, and that much is due to the Shell Company for so well organizing your supplies in most inaccessible parts of the desert.

Ettore Bugatti.

CHAPTER **13**

THE CROWNING ACHIEVE-MENT, "LA ROYALE"

The year 1929 would seem to have been a peak in Ettore Bugatti's career. Five years earlier, his Type 35 and then his Type 39 had brought him world renown; and his prestige had been strengthened in 1927 by the appearance of a Grand Sports model, the Type 43.[1] His racing successes had become too numerous to mention. In 1929 he won the grueling Targa Florio for the fifth successive year, and organized the second Bugatti Grand Prix for amateur owner-drivers.

Economic prosperity was still growing, and it seemed a time to embark on new and daring enterprises. So Bugatti produced his super-car, achieving his ambition and seeing a dream come true. It was the most elegant, luxurious, high-grade car ever to be produced, and was given the name *La Royale*—also known as the Golden Bug (because the prototype was much gilded).

Bugatti had long been thinking of a large, luxury production; he had referred to it in a letter to his friend Espanet in 1913, as mentioned earlier. The war came shortly after, and

(1) A straight-eight of 2,300 cc. (60 mm. x 100 mm.), three valves per cylinder. Accelerating to 90 mph. in 30 seconds, and easily reaching speeds of 100–112 mph., it is considered one of the four really great Bugatti models, with Types 23, 35 G.P. and 57.

the idea had to be abandoned. But in 1926, when his business was prospering again, he revived the project and, deriving his design from the aeroengines he had worked on, produced an impressive prototype. It had an engine of exceptional size and weighing seven cwt., with eight cylinders of 125 mm. x 150 mm. bore and stroke, giving a capacity of 14,726 cc. The engine developed 300 HP at 1,700 revolutions. The great size of the chassis (wheelbase of slightly more than 15 ft. and a track of 5 ft., 6 in.) enabled it to carry a comfortable seven-passenger body.[1]

When the first chassis was ready, Bugatti was so impatient to try it out that he did not wait for the body to be made. A few months previously he had bought a Packard "to see what it was made of," and now he simply had the body taken off that car and fitted to the Royale chassis; then he took it out on the road.

W. F. Bradley has written about going for a ride with Bugatti in this first Royale, while a guest at Molsheim. Bugatti was as pleased as a child with a new toy, driving at great speed and turning toward his passenger now and again, saying in English, "Good car, eh? Good car!"

Another day he proposed taking Costantini, Goux and Charavel for a drive in it. They all got in, Bugatti at the wheel, and set off along the road to Sainte Odile.

"The car was most comfortable," Charavel said later, "and held the road amazingly well, even at ninety miles an hour. But when the Guv'nor reached one hundred and ten I began to feel a little uneasy, because he hadn't driven so fast for a long time and I knew that we would soon come to a level-crossing with a right-hand bend directly afterwards. Well, he hadn't lost his touch! He was doing over a hundred, but he took the bend with the sureness of a professional. We

---

(1) The Royale was called Type 41. The gearbox was in the back axle, with a geared-down indirect gear for starting and a geared-up for fast running. The wheels were of special aluminum.

three passengers looked at each other feeling a lot more confident. On the straight, the three-ton Royale sped along at a hundred and twenty."

And so the builder of this prototype tried it out himself for several weeks, driving his favorite model over the mountain roads of Switzerland and northern Italy, and going down to the Pyrenees during the summer. The car gave him every satisfaction and proved to be one of the greatest achievements of his career. It climbed the narrow mountain roads easily, the engine never got overheated, not even in the hottest weather, and the smoothness of the gears and the amazing ease of handling this monster were equaled only by its strictly silent running.

But who would buy such perfection? The exceptional size of the engine and the refinements in the car's construction meant that the selling price was bound to be beyond the reach of the great majority of car-owners. By fixing the price of the chassis alone, without any bodywork, at half a million francs and giving an "unlimited guarantee," Bugatti confirmed the exceptional character of his latest creation.

He could see no point even in adding it to his catalogue. As his sales manager wrote to the representative of Prince Mohamed Abdel Said, who had shown some interest in the car: "For such a special chassis I have not considered it necessary to publish a catalogue. There is no need, in fact, of advertising a model for which the prospective buyers cannot be reached by the means adopted for standard cars."

Bugatti nevertheless thought the car should be brought to the attention of prospective buyers by means of a special leaflet describing its characteristic features, but written in a different style from an ordinary catalogue. So he organized a little competition among motoring correspondents (including the well-known Charles Faroux), and then invited them to Molsheim to choose the best text submitted. His idea was to have a general description of the car without too many technical terms, as these would mean little to the wealthy clientele forming the small market for the Royale. He left the journalists to decide among themselves, but before going from the room he produced a text from his pocket and added it to the others. It was unsigned, and all he told his guests was that he had not written it himself. The majority of the votes went to this text, however, and Bugatti then revealed to the surprised journalists that its author was his elder daughter, L'Ebé, and that she had avoided using technical terms because she did not understand them.

For the purpose, copies of this text were placed inside elegant, soft leather folders in "Bugatti blue," hand-sewn by the most skilful of the factory's leather craftsmen. The two bottom corners were given a silver facing, and the right-hand one bore the engraved signature of Ettore Bugatti. The text was as follows:

LA ROYALE

Prompt and flexible as a live creature, dependable and fast, powerful and silent, the Royale is a wonderful dream come true, made possible by thirty years' experience.

This car is a veritable synthesis of my experiments and my best products, and is a living mechanism.

The Royale is now perfect in all its details, and I am happy to say that, while giving it the most severe testing, I was constantly delighted with its wonderful mechanical behavior and with the evidence that it is well ahead of its time.

I have driven it over much of Europe in all weather and at all altitudes, without any sign of a defect.

The narrow roads over the Alps proved how flexible and easy to handle the Royale is, taking the sharp bends like a bicycle and remaining unaffected by variations in temperature.

This car is a pleasure to drive and takes all gradients in its stride, and is fast without ever giving an impression of effort.

The dimensions are undoubtedly the largest of any car,

and enable the chassis to be accommodated to the most diverse requirements. The most spacious and gracious coachwork would be a natural complement to the lines of the chassis, making a most harmonious and individualistic whole. The suspension, which is quite perfect, and the silence of the engine in low gear, have both aroused the greatest admiration.

The remarkable road-holding qualities—which are proverbial with Bugattis—make this wonderful thoroughbred extremely easy and docile to drive; and it can transport you anywhere, rapidly and powerfully, and in absolute safety, without giving the slightest apprehension.

In short, nothing has been left to chance; the smallest details have been minutely studied, each problem has been given the most careful attention.

The time has come when I believe I can consider this masterpiece of mechanical propulsion as completed and perfect, and I even venture to give it an unlimited guarantee.

This description is too summary for anyone to form an exact opinion of the merits of the Royale; a thorough trial run is necessary, in town, over mountains and on the flat. The imagination alone is incapable of grasping what this product represents in progress and perfection never before attained.

Molsheim, 1931.

In any event, no royal person ever owned a Royale. The car was thus named because Bugatti became acquainted with members of the Spanish royal family during the San Sebastian Grand Prix (in which Bugatti cars had some success), and he informed King Alfonso of the magnificent car which was then being built. The King expressed the wish to become the owner of the first completed chassis; but the monarchy was overthrown first.

The economic crisis in Europe, following the Wall Street crash of 1929, was fatal to the marketing of a car like the Royale. It was intended for a golden age which vanished as soon as the first few were built.

Bugatti had never thought of producing more than twenty to twenty-five Royales. As it turned out, only six or seven were built; and each has its history like any thoroughbred.

No. 1. The prototype (chassis No. 41100) was built in 1926–27 and was originally fitted with a Packard touring car body. It was subsequently re-bodied by Weymann and in 1929 obtained first prize at a *concours d' élégance* in Paris. It later met with an accident, and afterward was fitted with a fixed head coupé body (often called a coupé Napoleon) designed by Jean Bugatti. This car remained in the possession of the Bugatti family until acquired by the Alsatian collector, Schlumpf.

No. 2. This was the first chassis (No. 41111) to go to a client, being delivered as a two-seater roadster to the order of Mr. Armand Esders. There were no headlamps on it, because Mr. Esders had asked that none be fitted. "They would be of no use," he explained, "as I never drive at night." It was later re-bodied with a coupe de ville by the coachbuilder, Binder. It is now in the possession of Mr. William Harrah of Reno, Nevada.

No. 3. This car (chassis No. 41121) was ordered in 1930 by Dr. J. Fuchs, the German gynecologist, and delivered to him in 1931. It was fitted with a cabriolet body by the Munich coachbuilder, Ludwig Weinberger. Taken to the United States, it was saved from demolition in 1943 by Mr. C. A. Chayne, then chief engineer with General Motors Corporation. The car has been restored and is now in the Henry Ford Museum at Dearborn, Michigan.

No. 4. Chassis No. 41131 was delivered in 1933 to Captain C. W. Foster, who fitted it with an English Park-Ward four-door limousine body. He sent a report on it to Molsheim every Christmas until the war. In 1946 he sold the car to Mr. J. Lemon Burton, from whom it was bought by Schlumpf.

No. 5. This chassis (No. 41141) was fitted with a two-door sedan body by Kellner and remained in the possession of the Bugatti family for some time. It was exhibited at the 1932 Olympia Motor Show and listed at £6,500—more than double the price for the finest Rolls-Royce at the Show! It is now in the U.S.A., in the possession of Mr. Briggs Cunningham.

No. 6. Bugatti designed a four-door coupé body, known as a *berline de voyage,* for this chassis (No. 41150). The car is now in the U.S.A., another Royale owned by Mr. William Harrah.

THE PRICE OF BUGATTI CARS

For reasons already explained, Bugatti cars were relatively expensive. The following extracts from Bugatti catalogues issued from Molsheim in March, 1929, and May, 1938, give an idea of comparative prices of different types.

March, 1929

TOURING CARS

Chassis Type 44, 3-litre, 8-cylinder	60,000 Frs.
Chassis Type 40, 1.5-litre, 4-cylinder	36,500 Frs.
Torpedo body fitted to above chassis	39,000 Frs.

SPORTS CARS

Type 43, 2.3-litre, 8-cylinder, supercharged	130,000 Frs.
Type 38a, 2-litre, 8-cylinder, supercharged	75,000 Frs.

RACING CARS

Type 35b, 2.3-litre, 8-cylinder, supercharged	165,000 Frs.
Type 35c, 2-litre, 8-cylinder, supercharged	150,000 Frs.
Type 35a, 2-litre, 8-cylinder, unblown (imitation)	70,000 Frs.
Type 37a, 1.5-litre, 4-cylinder, supercharged	74,000 Frs.
Type 37, 1.5-litre, 4-cylinder, unblown	54,000 Frs.
Type 39, 1.5-litre, 8-cylinder, supercharged	165,000 Frs.

May 10, 1938

TOURING CARS

Chassis Type 57, 3.3-litre, straight-eight, twin-camshaft	73,000 Frs.
Same chassis with Ventoux body, 2-door, 4-seater	109,000 Frs.
Same chassis with Galibier saloon body, 2-door, 4-seater	113,000 Frs.
Same chassis with Stelvio cabriolet body, 2-door, 4-seater	111,000 Frs.
Same chassis with Atalante coupé body, 2-door, 2-seater	115,000 Frs.

GRAND TOURER

Chassis Type 57C, 3.3-litre, straight-eight, supercharged, twin-camshaft	90,000 Frs.

SPORTS CARS

Chassis Type 57S, 3.3-litre, straight-eight, twin-camshaft	100,000 Frs.
Same chassis with Atalante coupé body, 2-seater	140,000 Frs.
Same chassis with Atlantic coupé body, 2-seater	150,000 Frs.

GRAND SPORTS

Chassis Type 57C, 3.3-litre, supercharged, straight-eight, twin-camshaft	120,000 Frs.

The value of the franc having decreased by at least fifty times since 1929, it can be assumed that a Type 43 sports car would be priced today at six and a half million old francs (65,000 francs in 1967), the equivalent of nearly £5,000 or $13,000.

A comparison with English or American prices can only be very approximate, because of the difference in currency depreciation as compared with the franc and in the exchange rates. But it is interesting to note that the Type 44, 3-litre

(60,000 francs) was priced at the 1928 London Motor Show at £850. Again, the Type 57 Galibier saloon (113,000 francs) could be had at a chassis price of £590 in 1939, as against the £975 in 1936, because of the stronger exchange rate of the franc.

PART THREE:

The End of an Era

CHAPTER **14**

JEAN BUGATTI
AT MOLSHEIM

In 1928 Ettore Bugatti had produced the Royale for a European elite. In 1931 he used Royale engines as motive power for railcars.

This evolution marked both a great technical achievement and the end of an era. Bugatti was still to have many successes with his racing cars, however. In 1933, Varzi had a brilliant win at Monaco after a terrific battle with Nuvolari driving an Alfa Romeo. In 1934 Bugatti introduced his splendid Type 57, and in 1936 Wimille and Sommer won the French Grand Prix at Montlhéry.[1] The following year, Wimille partnered by Benoist carried off the Le Mans 24-Hours'.

But the days of luxurious limousines and semi-racing roadsters were over; and there was no market for extravagant Royales nor even for the minor Royales, the luxurious Types 46 and 50. In a world shaken by economic recession there was no place for a prince of automobiles.

So in 1931, faced with the precarious financial situation

(1) Driving a Type 57S, 3.3-litre. A week later, Wimille won the Rheims Grand Prix with the same car. In the autumn, he was second in the Vanderbilt Cup race at Long Island, averaging 65.9 mph. over this difficult and hilly course, finishing close behind the winner and in front of Nuvolari.

of his factory (due to the general regression in the car industry), Bugatti turned to rail locomotion. It was a time when techniques of road vehicles had outstripped those of railway engines, and the Guv'nor threw himself into the task with his usual enthusiasm. His employees backed him up, keen to prove themselves as competent to produce railcars as they had the motor cars which were a credit to their workmanship.

During the winter of 1932 Bugatti designed in all its details the railcar which later went into service on the French Railways and which benefited from a number of Bugatti patents. He was ill with influenza for much of that winter, and he worked in his bedroom at his Paris home (20, rue Boissière), using the mantelpiece as a table. In addition to designing the railcar, he mapped out the production program and planned the necessary alterations at the Molsheim factory and the means of getting the railcar to the Molsheim railway station.

Despite the many problems due to the change in production, the work went apace; there was no time to spare, for the western and eastern regions of the French Railways were expecting to put the new railcars into service that summer on the Paris-Deauville-Cabourg and the Paris-Strasbourg lines. But the drive at the factory was such that the prototype was ready before the lines had been laid between the factory and Molsheim railway station! However, Bugatti soon decided what to do. The railcar, equipped with bogies and wheels, was placed on a length of rail and pushed by manpower to the other end; then the rails were unbolted and relaid ahead . . . until Molsheim railway station, a mile and a half from the factory, was reached.

However, there were a number of hazards on the way, not the least being two sharp bends in the road. There was also the usual traffic, augmented by a long line of people all the way to the station who had come on foot and by bicycle to wait to see this "train" go by, giving encouragement but forming something of a hindrance.

The railcar was brought out of the factory gates at an angle, after part of the wall had been knocked down, so that it would be in line with the road. (Later, a turntable was installed at the exit.) The most difficult bend was at the approach to the square in front of the railway station. However, glasses of beer and sandwiches in great number were brought from the Hotel de la Gare to keep up morale; and with everyone helping, they finally hoisted the railcar onto the flat railway-truck on which it was taken to the official test track (Chartres-Gallardon).

This prototype passed all its tests successfully and was fitted out to carry passengers.[1] It ran daily on the Paris-Deauville-Cabourg line throughout the summer of 1933.

Later, two types of Bugatti railcars were in service. A light type (no trailer) using two Royale engines, and a "Presidential" (with single trailer) using four Royale engines. Jean Bugatti drove all the models on their official test runs.

In a newspaper of the time appeared the following report on a test run between Le Mans and Connerré, at which local authorities and representatives of the French Railways were present:

"M. Ettore Bugatti was present in person at the demonstration of the new, fine offspring from his factory. It is a railcar 72 feet long, mounted on two eight-wheel bogies. The wheels are insulated from the steel tire rims by a rubber layer—an invention of the constructor—and the bogies themselves are fully sprung and so mounted as to give a comfortable ride. In addition to all these qualities, the bogies are so made that a piece of line ten to twenty inches long

(1) 84 seated and 23 standing. Two engines, 400 HP. Cruising speed, 70 mph.; top speed of over 90 mph. It reached 60 mph. in 1 min., 43 secs., and 70 in 2 min., 12 secs. At a speed of 65 it could brake to a stop within 300 yards.

could be removed without the railcar being in danger of derailment.

"Motive power is given by four 8-cylinder Bugatti engines each of 250 HP. There is no gearbox, but all the engines give full power whatever the speed. The driver is in a central, raised cabin; the controls are simple, and a double braking system is powerful enough to bring the railcar to a halt in a very short distance.

"The fifteen-mile test run was covered at an average speed of 106 mph., thus beating the record of 99 mph. held by a German railcar on the Berlin-Hamburg run.

"The railcar, which was driven by M. Jean Bugatti, was said by the technicians present to hold the rails remarkably well."

At a later date, on December 16, 1935, Jean Bugatti drove one of the 400 HP railcars on the Strasbourg-Paris run of 313 miles in 3 h., 30 mins., an average speed of 90 mph., and a world record for a long-distance run. Shortly afterwards, a Bugatti railcar set up a world speed record of 122 mph., timed over six miles.[1]

Some eighty Bugatti railcars were in service on the French Railways for twenty years or so. The last of them were withdrawn in 1958, and these had been in use since 1937.

The development and production of these railcars resulted in Ettore Bugatti being absent from Molsheim for long periods, for he was obliged to maintain close contact with the engineers and administrators of the French Railways. From 1931 onward, most of his time was spent in Paris. His son, Jean, thus became gradually responsible for the Molsheim factory, but this was a natural evolution for Bugatti had prepared his son for the task by associating him with both the experimental and the production side of the factory.

(1) When brakes were applied at 93 mph. the railcar was brought to a stop in a little over 800 yards—a record unbeaten until 1964.

When Jean was eighteen he drove all the models, and there was nothing he did not know about their construction. Two years later, he was helping to tune the engines and to test the new models. It was a natural consequence for him to have a large part in developing the railcar prototype, and to drive it during tests and for a period in the summer of 1933. He was subsequently responsible for the three types of Bugatti railcars: the light type (two engines), the double type (four engines) with single trailer, and the triple version with trailer back and front.

Certain unexpected circumstances, however, had speeded up this process whereby the management of the Molsheim factory passed from father to son. A happy working atmosphere had long existed at the factory, thanks to the special relationship between Ettore Bugatti and his employees. He was aware of the progress of the trade union movement in France, but was somewhat perplexed by its development and demands.

He had, in his particular way, already introduced a system of social benefits among his employees in the years 1929–30. He considered them to be quite well paid and enjoying various advantages, and so expected them to have savings or to be improving their living conditions. If not, it could only be due to bad management or wasteful habits. He, therefore, decided to encourage thrift by increasing the wages of workmen who could prove they were living within their means and either putting money by or acquiring possessions. It was a most delicate matter and a difficult scheme to put into operation, even among a small body of country-bred people and in the exceptional conditions of a factory run on artisanal methods.

However, Ettore Bugatti gave up some of his time to be available in his office, about once a week, to those of his employees who wished to take advantage of his offer and who were prepared to reveal their financial situation; that is to say, the property or possessions they had acquired (land, a house, furniture, etc.) *since* starting to work at the Bugatti factory. The Guv'nor showed his appreciation of such efforts by signing a payment order which could be cashed at the cashier's office, without any explanation being required. Secrecy was thus guaranteed, and this reassured those who were hesitant to divulge their financial situation and possessions. The cashier was the trusted M. Pracht, whom everyone looked upon as a friend and counselor, so all went well. Nevertheless, it was not a system that could spread very far, despite the generosity and wisdom behind it. The Guv'nor ended by smiling at it himself.

It was then that the labor unrest in France developed into strike action. In 1936 one big factory after another was affected and brought to a standstill. Bugatti thought his was safe from trouble. "I've nothing to worry about," he kept saying. "My workpeople know me; they're part of the family."

But the impossible happened. The men stopped work, there were protest marches, the Red Flag was waved and the factory was occupied for a sit-down strike. It was a terrible shock, a thunderclap without a storm. Bugatti was embittered by what he took to be so much ingratitude and an attack on him personally. He left Molsheim altogether; and so it was that Jean, then aged twenty-six, took over entirely.

Until his death in 1939, Jean was in complete charge of a factory employing 1,200 to 1,400 men. He often had long telephone conversations with his father in the evenings, and he saw him in Paris now and again; but all that was only moral support, and the effective management of the factory fell on Jean's shoulders.

The late 1930s were a fruitful period for new Bugatti models, and Jean was responsible for producing Types 57,

59, 50B, 57S, 45, 64, and others. He also fitted engines to speed-boats with which Ettore Bugatti won several events, and he built the aeroengines for the fighter monoplane which his father designed in 1938. Jean often worked well into the night testing engines or tuning racing cars, which he drove on the roads around Molsheim. By day, there were the many responsibilities of management, for he preferred not to delegate these burdens any more than he did the testing of new models.

Early in 1937 he succeeded in obtaining the agreement of the trade unions for the ban on overtime to be lifted temporarily at the factory, to enable the cars entered for the Le Mans 24-Hours' to be got ready in time. It was eleven years since French cars had been successful in this great international event. The negotiations with the trade unions were conducted at the highest level, and much patience and tact were required by Jean in order to have his factory exempted from the general ban on overtime. The talks were also an indication of how things had changed. In the past, the Guv'nor and the workmen would have decided between themselves on the extra hours to be worked; now the decision was made by an organization far removed from the factory, but which was, nevertheless, aware of the national prestige involved.

The intensive efforts made at the factory resulted in a popular win for one of the 3.3-litre Bugattis, Type 57, driven by Robert Benoist and Jean-Pierre Wimille at an average speed of 85.13 mph.

Roger Labric reported on the event as follows:

"Before a record crowd, and in very thundery weather, the start of the 24-Hours' was given on Saturday, June 19th, to forty-eight cars. The Bugatti entries, driven by Benoist/Wimille and Labric/Veyron, bore witness to the great effort made by the Molsheim manufacturer. They were both of

the famous Type 57, one of Ettore Bugatti's finest achievements, and had been given a "tank," streamlined body; their
road-holding qualities were remarkable.

"The race was hotly disputed, but in spite of the heavy
rainstorms on the Saturday evening, the leading drivers
never decreased speed for a moment, to the great joy of the
massed and enthusiastic crowds.

"The lap record was constantly broken, first by the
Bugatti drivers, then by Dreyfus, Brunet and Paul Delahaye;
until the skillful Wimille set up the new record of 96.3 mph.
late on the Sunday morning. However, this furious rate led
to the retirement of a great number of cars, and toward the
end only seventeen still remained in the race. At four o'clock
on Sunday afternoon, with the sun blazing down, the No. 2
Bugatti crossed the finishing line more than sixty miles
ahead of its nearest rival. The co-drivers, Wimille and
Benoist, were given a great ovation by the crowd.

"Then, in the almost religious silence which followed the
announcement of the result, the *Marseillaise* was played
here for the first time since 1926. The emotion which was
felt soon gave way to joyous scenes at the success of the national colors and our regained prestige.

"Ettore Bugatti had once again given France one of the
finest successes in motoring history. By winning the Cup,
Wimille and Benoist had not only set up a record for the
distance covered as well as a new lap record, but also had
taken first position in the qualifying tests for 1938. Their
success could not have been more complete or clear-cut. It
confirms the wonderful technical skill of Bugatti and the outstanding class of Robert Benoist and Jean-Pierre Wimille."

The win at Le Mans caused general delight at Molsheim,
especially because everyone was happy to see a return to the
great successes of the past.

But there were difficult times ahead for Jean Bugatti, due

to the economic recession, increased taxation, and the need to adapt to the changing demands. His understanding and hard work enabled him to put the factory on a new footing. He had, after all, gained all his technical knowledge at the factory and knew every stage of production, knew the work performed by each craftsman.[1] He had grown up with the business—a business made of complexities, of successes and failures, and of financial and human difficulties. All of this had given Jean a balanced, calm outlook, stripped of youthful illusions and free of hasty judgments. His future appeared most promising and bright.

The memory of this handsome young man with laughing blue eyes and a frank look, kind, witty and elegant, is still very much alive. Old employees still speak of him with emotion, which is the best of all tributes to this young life so rich in promise and so abruptly ended.

Jean met with a fatal accident on August 11, 1939, while testing the car which had won the Le Mans 24-Hours' and was entered for the Grand Prix at La Baule.[2] It happened at about ten that evening. He went out after dinner with the family, saying "I'll be back in fifteen minutes" in answer to our warnings to be careful.

He was going to test the car over a long, straight stretch of the tree-lined road to Strasbourg. It began just outside Molsheim, and there were helpers posted at either end to control the traffic. Jean's younger brother, Roland, was at the start with a few workmen to warn cars, and a few factory employees were at the far end to stop oncoming traffic for a few minutes. A few cars drew onto the verges to watch. Jean drove full out along the straight, confident that he had the

(1) Ettore Bugatti did not entirely approve of the technical training in state schools, believing it to be based too much on established practices and set rules, thereby curbing the creative imagination of young craftsmen.

(2) Type 57G, 3.3-litre unblown, "tank" body.

road to himself. Suddenly a cyclist popped out and began to cross. Jean braked hard, swerved and hit a tree, killing himself outright. He was crushed against the wheel.

Our father was in Brussels, and the news of Jean's death came as a terrible shock to him. My mother had recently been operated on by Professor Leriche, who feared that the blow to her might be too much; but she showed admirable courage and was, in fact, an example to us all. Her calm resignation was a source of strength in our bereavement.

The young and impetuous cyclist received only a few cuts and bruises, thanks to Jean's sacrifice. But he was haunted by the thought of having caused Jean's death, and three years later he committed suicide.

THE BUGATTI RAILCAR

M. Domboy, a highly qualified engineer who had received his early training in Paris, joined the Bugatti firm in 1932. He was, for many years, the close assistant of Ettore Bugatti, who used to give him his own drawings and sketches to examine before they were sent to the drawing office.

M. Domboy was naturally the person to whom I turned for a detailed and technical description of my father's railcars, aeroplanes and yacht. This report is much too long and technical to be printed in full in the present biography. It was deposited with the Bugatti Owners' Club in London, where it can be consulted. Some extracts from the section on railcars follow. (Details of Ettore Bugatti's yacht and of his many patents are included in the Appendices.)

"Ettore Bugatti always made a point of checking the capabilities of his cars and other machines, and by very simple processes of calculation. He had constantly in mind the dimensions of his machine tools and the various possibilities they allowed. Whenever he designed new machine tools or adapted existing ones, it was only after much thought and experiment; there was never any question of improvising.

"In all cases, he insisted on deciding the working range of each part, himself. His great attention to this matter is obvious from the many marginal notes and indications he made on the detailed drawings relating to the different stages in the production of a car part. In addition, the Guv'nor designed the chief machine tools and handed his drawings to one of the draftsmen to be worked on or sent them direct to the machine shop. He would never examine or even accept documents relating to another person's invention unless it was protected by patent. He made no exception to this line of conduct, which showed how punctilious he was in regard to the work of others.

"The Guv'nor's projects relating to rail locomotion date back to 1931, and they resulted in a number of patents of high technical value and which were at once developed industrially. They included:

"(a) Various models of wheels with insulating rubber layers (ten patents taken out in the major European countries between 1932 and 1934),

"(b) Fully-sprung bogies mounted on four axles.

"The Bugatti bogie varied with the type of railcar but always had four axles.

"His invention solved the problem of stability and greatly improved the safety of rail locomotion. His bogies were so mounted as to give safety and an excellent ride; it was impossible for any bogie wheels to slip from the rails. The weight was evenly distributed over the four axles, and perfect stability was assured when the track made a curve.

"The first tests of the prototype, later known as the Presidential type, took place in 1933 over a section of track (Chartres-Gallardon) which was used only for testing rolling stock. A speed limit of 59 mph. was in force because of the poor state of the track. But on its first run the prototype, driven by Jean Bugatti, reached a speed of more than 76 mph. The railway technicians who were riding in it could hardly believe their eyes when they saw this speed registered on the Flaman, the meter used on French locomotives. After some hesitation, which was fully justified, they agreed to continue the test run up to a maximum speed of 83 mph.

"Their colleagues on the P.L.M. (Southern) line had a similar experience a little later, when the railcar was making test runs in the region of Fontainebleau. It crossed the viaduct, which is built in a long curve, at a speed of 108 mph.

"These and many other demonstrations definitely established the superiority of the Bugatti railcars in matters of safety.

"Other Bugatti patents in this connection were: seven relating to a reversible seat (1932–33) and three on improvements to it (1933); seven relating to the means of coupling a trailer to the railcar (1936–37)."

AN APPRECIATION OF JEAN BUGATTI

M. Domboy, who worked in close cooperation with Jean Bugatti ever since joining the firm, has kindly written the following appreciation.

"He was a young man—one might even say very young—who was known to everyone at the factory, but whose air of responsibility and authority marked him out as the head of it. He was one of those who could make great demands on his associates because he possessed to a high degree the gift for arousing enthusiasm, the urge to create, and faith in ultimate success. But it is not enough just to describe Jean Bugatti's influence on his staff, unless the reasons for it, being so strong, are understood.

"Jean Bugatti mastered all the problems that beset the manufacturer of cars and railcars. His powers of observation were highly developed, and he was able to see many things that escaped the notice of less observant people—that is to say, the majority.

"However, there are not many people who are capable

of drawing the correct conclusions from what they have observed. Jean Bugatti was one of those rare persons who are not deceived by appearances; and in analyzing mechanical and physical phenomena he did not commit the error of confusing cause and effect—an error which is often made and leads to bad mistakes.

"These aptitudes were of great assistance to him when tuning up engines, which he began to do before he was even twenty years of age.

"It was surprising to see such a young man doing this rough and often dangerous work, very different from the usual occupations of men of his age. This can be explained only by the fact that Jean Bugatti was very mature for his years, and by the influence his father had over him from an early age.

"He also had a very keen, practical sense which enabled him to avoid the traps into which many an inventor's imagination leads. Although endowed with just as lively an imagination as his father, he nevertheless remained close to reality and kept in touch with the men when in charge of the factory.

"There was a mutual understanding between him and his co-workers, largely because he let pass no opportunity to find out what was worrying them and what difficulties they were encountering in their work; and he was interested to hear their ideas, whether good or bad, and to listen to their ambitions and their hopes for the firm's future.

"This was one of Jean Bugatti's most attractive features. He had soon learned to form his own opinion of men and not to be influenced by words and deeds which did not spring from their real character.

"It was not a question of distrust, such as one finds in jealous and suspicious natures. But once he had summed up a man, he stuck to his opinion of him. Once he had put his trust in a man, it was for good; conversely, if he had decided that a man was not worthy of his confidence, there was no hope of the man ever gaining it. In the former event, he showed his confidence on every possible occasion; this was much appreciated by good workers, who were undoubtedly in the majority.

"Jean Bugatti brought to his day-to-day work a decisive mind which sprang partly from his character but also resulted from his experiences as a racing driver.

"During recent years, when the fate of the firm has hung in the balance, we have often thought of him and wondered what he would have done if he were still with us; for we had so much faith in him.

"This brings me to the tragic night of his death. Only those who knew the firm before 1939 can realize what it suffered by this loss. They are the only ones, too, who have any real conception of the example handed down by the man who, after the Guv'nor, was both the brain and soul of the business.

"He will never be forgotten. He has left the memory of a helmeted and white-clad knight at the wheel of a racing car, allied with that of a real head of an industry, of a great engineer and a big-hearted man."

CHAPTER **15**

THE SECOND FLIGHT
FROM MOLSHEIM

Less than a month after the tragic death of Jean Bugatti, the Second World War began. And, as in 1914, Ettore Bugatti chose to serve France. Not for a moment did he imagine otherwise—despite the fact that he was still of Italian nationality and Mussolini had a pact with Hitler. During the "phony war" he evacuated his factory to Bordeaux, in conditions of indescribable difficulty, and turned it over to work of national importance. The German invasion and subsequent capitulation of France brought an end to his business, for the factory was taken over by the Germans and he was obliged to sell out. After the war, in order to have the business and premises restored to him, a court action became necessary.

It would be best to let Ettore Bugatti speak for himself in this matter. At the beginning of 1945 he drew up a memorandum to support his claim for the restitution of his factory; it was more or less a summary of his life's work, and so is here reproduced in full even though the earlier part contains details already known to the reader.

Written without bitterness and in a calm tone, this memorandum typifies the generous and clearsighted nature of the Guv'nor, and his determination when up against injustice.

He had never thought of becoming a naturalized Frenchman, not even when it might have been in his own interest,
for both his career and his patriotism had, in themselves,
shown him to be French at heart. However, he applied for
French citizenship and obtained his naturalization papers
on February 25, 1946—a little more than a year before his
death.

But why so late in life? His children were French. The
answer is that he thought it in poor taste to change what
nature had made him. He had been born in Italy of Italian
parents, and although they had nearly always lived in France
he disliked the idea of disavowing his origins. He looked
upon Italy and France as a son of well-bred parents thinks of
his mother and father. It was a noble conception, but
brought much worry and difficulty into his life and twice contributed to his ruin.

The document, dated from Paris on April 3, 1945, read
as follows:

"It pains me to have to justify my past as a car manufacturer. I will be short and refer to the chief stages in a career
which was closely connected with the history of locomotion.

"In 1902 I sold a manufacturing license to one of the
world's leading firms of car manufacturers at that time—the
De Dietrich firm, of which the head was then Baron Eugène
de Dietrich. As I was still under age, my father signed the
contract. I spent nearly all my time in Alsace, supervising
construction of the cars, and also produced five other types
of cars for this firm, one of which was a racing car for the
Paris-Madrid race (bore and stroke of 160 mm. x 160 mm.,
weight one ton) and built under my supervision by the
Société Alsacienne de Construction Mécanique at Graffenstaden.

"In 1910 I started up a Bugatti factory at Molsheim and
built the first small car of 1,100 cc. *in series production.*

Among other details, this car had a 4-cylinder engine and four gears.

"At various times I sold licenses to other car manufacturers and to governments:

"Two types of 'Baby-Peugeot' cars, one a two-seater, the other a four-seater, before 1914.

"Three types of cars to the Deutz Gaz Motor Fabrik, one having an engine with 120 mm. bore, the second with 140 mm. bore, and the third with chain drive.

"Two types of cars to the English firm of Crossley.

"Three types of cars to the Diatto firm in Turin, and two aeroengines in 1916 (one a straight-eight cylinder with a reduction gear, the other a 16-cylinder double-bank).

"By 1914 my *marque* had a world-wide reputation. On the declaration of war I abandoned all I possessed at Molsheim and came to put myself at the disposition of France. I concentrated my activities chiefly on aircraft and particularly on aeroengines.

"A group of American experts, after visiting several of the Allied countries, came to Paris and the head of the mission, the well-known aircraft constructor, Howard Marmon, arranged for my aeroengine to be purchased by the American government. This was the only engine to be produced by the American government under a European license, five thousand being made in the first instance (ten thousand were in course of production when the end of the war came).

"The French government also purchased a license and arranged for production of this aeroengine by the Peugeot firm. It was a 16-cylinder double-bank 400 HP design, with a reduction gear and layout enabling a 37 mm. cannon to be fired through the propeller shaft. The whole construction was protected by patents until 1935. This type of aeroengine gave birth to the Bréguet in France, the Napier in England and the Mann in Germany, as well as to many other aeroengines in U-form or H-form.

"The test runs were quite conclusive. This aeroengine was the first in France to undergo a successful test run of ten hours, followed by another endurance test of fifty hours in 1917 which was also successful and the first of its kind.

"My constructions showed the successful use of a reduction gear, the only one at that time to have given satisfaction and demonstrated the usefulness of this device.

"When Italy entered the war I was mobilized in France at the request of the Technical Section.

"At the end of hostilities I went back to Alsace, which was French once more. My Molsheim factory had been rightly considered as capable of producing precision work of high standard, and so much of the machinery had been removed to Germany, while the factory itself had suffered considerable damage.

"Despite my attitude during the war, and the position I had assumed well before Italy entered the war on the side of the Allies, the French government refused to pay me war-damages because of my nationality. I applied to the Italian government, which also refused to pay because my property and my factory were in a foreign country.

"However, through my knowledge and my work, Molsheim became a factory with a high reputation again and my products were renowned the world over. They were protected by many patents filed in France and other countries, patents which contributed to the general advancement both during and after their period of legal existence. I give as an example the hydraulic brakes which were exhibited at the first post-war Motor Show as being one of my inventions.

"My cars had a unique record of racing successes, which were always French successes, competing against teams of French and foreign cars of all firms, large and small. Altogether I won more than ten thousand races with my cars and established thirty-seven international records which were still standing in 1939, many of them having been made in inter-

Type 43, supercharged straight-eight 2.3 litre.

Type 57, Atalante coupé—one of the most original of all Bugatti bodies. (*H. G. Conway*)

Before the start of the French Grand Prix, 1931, Bugatti gives his final instructions to Varzi. (*Bibl. Nat.*)

The car with which Wimille won the Prisoners of War Cup in 1946—Bugatti's last great success. (*Mlle. Bugatti*)

Wimille driving a Type 57S at Montlhéry, 1936. (*H. G. Conway*)

Type 57S, Atalante coupé—one of the most famous Bugatti tourers. (*H. G. Conway*)

Ettore Bugatti in a relaxed moment. (*Mlle. Bugatti*)

Type 59, the last of the great Bugatti racing cars. This one was bought by Earl Howe in 1934 and won the 500 miles race at Brooklands the following year.

national Grand Prix events organized by the Automobile Clubs of the major European countries.

"As a constructor of railcars, I held the world speed record of 122 mph., timed over six miles; also the world record for a long-distance run—an average speed of 90 mph. over the Strasbourg-Paris run of 313 miles, covered in 3 hours, 30 minutes.

"As a constructor of speed-boats, I held several world records. At the time, I could build only boats which it was possible to transport from Molsheim by rail. However, at my experimental workshop in Paris, I produced a very light motor-torpedo-boat which could reach a speed of 80 mph.

"The outbreak of war prevented me from setting up a new world speed record with the airplane which the Minister for Air had specially commissioned. It was ready in August, 1939, and ought to have greatly exceeded the existing all-class record of 500 mph. Its design included a number of innovations which have since been adopted in combat planes.

"The war did not cause me to change my opinions or attitude. A proof of this is the transfer of my factory to Bordeaux soon after war was declared. The operation cost me millions of francs which were never refunded, for the only payment I received was for the expenses incurred in the actual transport. Breakages, the destruction of installations, etc., were never taken into account. These losses amounted to at least fifteen per cent of the value of the machinery, which meant twenty to twenty-five million francs in 1939.

"In addition to the work under government contract (crankshafts and various components for Hispano-Suiza engines), I designed and began on my own initiative to make some special lathes for the manufacture of the Hispano-Suiza crankshafts. These lathes would have enabled a crankshaft to be made in twice forty-five minutes. The arrival of the enemy in Bordeaux brought all this work to a halt.

"From then on, and because of my nationality, my position became very difficult. My refusal to obey the pressing demands of the German authorities to return to Alsace resulted in their taking over the machinery and all the material at Bordeaux and expelling me from the factory.

"During the next two years, while under pressure and threats of all kinds, ruined, yet not wanting to produce anything on the enemy's behalf and wishing at all costs to keep the employees who had remained loyal to me, I contracted debts amounting to more than ten million francs.

"At the same time, a more serious and direct threat was hanging over me. The authorities announced that my property in Alsace would be put up for sale to meet my overdraft at the bank in Strasbourg and debts to various suppliers. This sale stripped me of everything in return for thirty million francs—a very small sum for a factory where fifteen hundred workmen could produce in their entirety constructions recognized as being of the highest quality.

"Nevertheless, I made no approach to the German authorities nor sought any support from them. At official inquiries, which I was obliged to attend, a member of the French Organizing Committee for Automobiles was always present. Although my firm was considered to be French, there was no legal way of reaching an agreement. A French person was not allowed to sell, and an Italian had no claim to compensation.

"Such was the position when a compromise solution was put before me. I was obliged, in the face of threats, to accept a sum of 150 million francs against the surrender of my factory; this sum was much below the real value, which was estimated at 334 million francs on December 1, 1941.

"This compulsory sale destroyed nearly half a century's work. Still, the balance is owing to me by virtue of a requisition order, and the documents in justification of this are on file at the Préfecture in Bordeaux. The sale was made with the knowledge of the Organizing Committee for Automobiles, in agreement with the Ministry for Industrial Production.

"Although not wishing to impose myself, I take note of the desire expressed by the Molsheim town council and declare that I am quite prepared to acquire the Molsheim factory again, on financial terms still to be arranged.

"I am, of course, ready to carry out any contract work which the government might decide to entrust to me, just as I was at the beginning of the war, when I transferred my factory to Bordeaux to make Hispano-Suiza crankshafts. I should also be able to carry on with my post-war program, of which I give an outline below; my inactivity during the past few years has enabled me to complete the study and preparation of it:

"Precision machine tools (milling and perforating machinery).

"Special machinery for ship building (machines for bending and shaping steel plates, for chamfering, riveting, etc.).

"A small two-seater tourer, 4-cylinder 300 cc. supercharged engine.

"A 4.5-litre car designed in 1939.

"A sports car and a racing car with 8 and 16 cylinders, respectively, and of 1,500 cc. capacity.

"Diesel boat engines of 100, 200 and 300 HP.

"When I first set up in business at Molsheim in 1910, the population was barely one thousand. In 1939 the factory, which I had built up, was employing fifteen hundred people and Molsheim had a population of more than four thousand.

"The growth of Molsheim is due entirely to the work at my factory, for the other localities in the region have not developed in a like manner. I built up with my own money, gained by my own work, an industrial concern which was equipped with more than 850 machine tools, the great majority of them recently developed and the most perfect of their kind, such as very few factories in France had in use.

"I submit that my efforts and the resulting production gave my firm the highest reputation, and it would be most regrettable if this firm, which has constantly been a credit to France, were not allowed to start up again in the place where it was created.

"(signed)   Ettore Bugatti,

"Paris, April 3, 1945."

This statement was drawn up and submitted during the long negotiations which eventually led to Ettore Bugatti taking legal action to recover his property from the Administration des Domaines (a state office). At the court hearing (at Saverne, in the Bas-Rhin), various interested parties introduced side issues, and the result was that Bugatti lost his case. His lawyers appealed against the decision, and the case was taken to the Court of Appeal at Colmar.

Counsel for parties hostile to Bugatti made violent speeches which were a great emotional shock to him and caused a nervous breakdown. But his own advocates[1] were armed with indisputable documents and obtained judgment for him, dated June 11, 1947, whereby the Molsheim factory and property were legally restored to their founder and rightful owner.

THE GERMANS AT MOLSHEIM (1940–44)

During the German occupation of France the Molsheim factory was taken over by a German industrialist, Trippel, and was called the Trippel Werke.

Before the war, Trippel had been making amphibious vehicles at his factory at Homberg, in the Saar. These vehicles were used on large estates and for forestry work, for shooting, fishing, etc., but they were chiefly intended for

(1) Me. Rengade, legal and financial consultant from Paris; Me. Weiller, of the Strasbourg Bar, and Me. Sinay, of the Colmar Bar.

military purposes. Proof of this is the great increase in their production which took place after war was declared in 1939.

After the collapse of France in June, 1940, the Germans occupied much of the country, including the Bordeaux region. At the end of July, Trippel arrived at the Bugatti factory on the Boulevard Alfred Daney at Bordeaux to obtain possession of all the machines and material which had been transported from Molsheim soon after the declaration of war.

Trippel had already succeeded, with the support of the German authorities, in obtaining entrance to the Bugatti premises at Molsheim, and had transferred workmen, machinery and materials there from his factory at Homberg. His task was made all the easier by the fact that he stood very high with the Nazis (it was whispered that he was on intimate terms with Himmler). He held the rank of Obersturmbannführer and wore on his uniform the emblem of a member of the Führerstab (Hitler's Advisory Staff).

A number of Bugatti workmen were tracked down through the Labor Office in Molsheim and requisitioned for work at the factory, forming a core for the unskilled labor which was brought in from elsewhere. In the first half of October, 1940, the machine tools from Bordeaux began to arrive at Molsheim. These removals continued throughout the winter, and included a considerable amount of raw material.

In 1941 the Kriegsmarine took over part of the factory with a view to making torpedoes. It set up the Maschinenfabrik Molsheim as a separate organization, while the production of amphibious vehicles remained under Trippel. A wall was built dividing the factory in two and keeping the adversaries apart. This situation—Trippel (Nazi Party) on one side, the Maschinenfabrik Molsheim (Kriegsmarine) on the other—lasted until the spring of 1942. Then the German Air Ministry—the sole customer for the torpedoes being produced at Molsheim—put everything under one control. The dividing wall was demolished when General Milch, Inspector-General of the Luftwaffe, visited the factory, and at the same time a Trippel Company was formed; the Nazis had the upper hand again. A relative calm was established in the running of the factory, and this was used to install new machine tools and to sell the Bugatti machinery considered to be of no use to the production program.

In 1944 there were about 1,800 people employed at the factory, of whom 150 were Russian POW.

The monthly production target was 150 torpedoes and 20 amphibious vehicles.

Other productions included several snowplows, a prototype of a motor-driven sled for use on the Russian steppes, a number of sleds with closed bodywork for transporting the wounded, some hundreds of flying bombs (V.1s), and a prototype of an armored amphibious vehicle.

This amphibious vehicle had a 2.5-litre 6-cylinder Opel engine, a four-speed gearbox and a collapsible propeller. Maximum speed on land was 50 mph.

CHAPTER **16**

DEATH OF ETTORE BUGATTI

"There is nothing which we know everything about," René Leriche used to say.[1] "Only facts count. And even then, you have to know what to look for."

Ettore Bugatti knew that instinctively; his well-known reserve was a proof of it, as was his prudence when confronted with the surprises and the unexpected resulting from progress. Throughout his life, he knew full well how to observe and to draw conclusions, to put them into effect, without ever pretending to have solved anything.

The Guv'nor disliked people talking about "Bugatti's genius," and so the term has not been used in this biography, out of respect for his wishes. It has often been applied, however, by eminent writers who liked his strong character and personality, his good nature and interest in everything to do with life.

By a final irony of fate, it was while the ownership of his factory was being disputed that Bugatti had a brilliant win on his own ground—which was different from that of his judges.

The first major motor racing event in France after the war was the Grand Prix de la Libération, which was held

(1) René Leriche, an eminent surgeon and a professor at the Collège de France, died on December 28, 1955. He and Ettore Bugatti were close friends for many years. Their wives, too, had much in common, and were intelligent companions to these two outstanding men.

in the Bois de Boulogne, over a temporary circuit, on September 9, 1946. There were three races:

1. The Prisoners of War Cup, for cars of more than 3-litre capacity.
2. The Liberation Cup, for supercharged 1.5-litre sports cars.
3. The Robert Benoist Cup, for 1,100 cc. cars.

There were sixteen starters for the Prisoners of War Cup (5 Buggatis, 7 Delahayes, 2 Talbots, 1 Alfa and 1 Maserati), and it was won by Wimille in a Bugatti, with a time of 1 h., 3 min., 33 secs., and an average speed of 70 mph. The car, which was the fastest ever built by Ettore Bugatti, was a supercharged 4.7-litre 8-cylinder with bore and stroke of 84 mm. x 107 mm. It weighed 17 cwt. and could reach a speed of 185 mph.

For the Parisians, deprived of motor-racing spectacles for six or seven years, it was a great return to other days and the win was loudly acclaimed. For Ettore Bugatti, it was a farewell to the racing scene, though he was unaware of this at the time.

Seven months later, in April, 1947, he caught a chill while returning by car to Paris, the evening of the end of the hearing of his appeal before the Colmar court. He was exhausted and in low spirits; he developed influenza, then an obstructed artery left him half-paralyzed. He lingered on for four months, and despite the care of specialists gradually sank into a coma and died on August 21, 1947, at the American Hospital in Neuilly. He was sixty-six years of age.

He was thus deprived of the joy of seeing his factory returned to the Bugatti family.[1]

(1) Barbara Bugatti had died on July 21, 1944, after a painful illness. There were four children from the marriage: L'Ebé, Lidia (Madame de Boigne), Jean (accidentally killed, August 11, 1939), and Roland.

Ettore married again, his second wife being Geneviève Delcuze, of whom he had a daughter, Thérèse, and a son, Michel.

His funeral took place at the church of St. Pierre-de-Chaillot, his parish church, which was filled with mourners. A final farewell to him was given on behalf of the French Automobile Club by the chairman of its Sports Committee, M. de Peyerimhoff.

Ettore Bugatti, grand officer of the Corona d'Italia, officer of the Légion d'Honneur, is buried in the family vault at Dorlisheim, not far from the factory to which he devoted much of his life.

AN APPRECIATION OF ETTORE BUGATTI

The last page has been reached in the account of Ettore Bugatti's life, a life full of joys and tribulations, in which intelligence and a creative imagination brought into being many odd but practical inventions.

By keeping to facts, I have tried to portray the Guv'nor and his strong and attractive personality.

A testimony of friendship which would have touched Ettore Bugatti very much comes from his great friend the Duc de Gramont, whose recollections round off this biography. They reveal little-known details of the family life at Molsheim, which was both the background and framework of Ettore Bugatti's whole existence, of his enthusiasms and strivings for progress.

The Duc de Gramont wrote as follows:

"I first met Ettore Bugatti in 1914. From the very outset, I was impressed by the strength of his creative imagination. Our first meeting was at Chalais-Meudon. I had been recalled from the front in order to do research on combat planes, which were in their infancy and presented many problems. Ettore Bugatti, who was then aged thirty-two, often came to see me there.

"He was full of original ideas which, although daring, were nevertheless practical. With selfless enthusiasm, he brought to France, the country of his adoption, the fruits of his wide experience in engine design and layout. Much of his youth had been spent in Paris, where his father had had a workshop and made furniture to his own design. But young Bugatti was attracted by mechanics, which he saw and felt to be an art; and he worked as a draftsman for the Deutz Motors firm. Later, in 1910, he set up his own factory at Molsheim, on the advice of his industrialist friends who were reckoning on France recovering Alsace-Lorraine in the near future. On the outbreak of war he returned to Paris, where Major Doran, who was in charge of the Aeronautical Technical Section, gave him a warm welcome and explained the kind of aeroengine needed.

"One of Bugatti's designs was for a 16-cylinder doublebank engine with a layout enabling a cannon to be fired through the propeller shaft; this synchronizing of the firing of the cannon with the turn of the propeller-blades had presented many difficult problems.

"Bugatti had no workshop in Paris, so he began to assemble his first aeroengine in my laboratory at Levallois-Perret.

"After the war, he started on the brilliant career that is known to everybody, with his remarkable racing cars and numerous successes in events the world over. It finally seemed quite natural for him always to take the leading places. And this was all accomplished by his own means.

"However, one cannot write of Ettore Bugatti and confine oneself to this one aspect of what can properly be called his genius. In order to know the whole man, he had to be seen at Molsheim, in the large industrial concern that was his own creation and in his charming house set in its own grounds just beyond the factory, on the road to Colmar. There he came into his own—before his voluntary exile in Paris at the time of the 1936 strikes, which had greatly distressed him. And he was a very different man from what most people imagined.

"On leaving the factory, which was constantly being altered and extended, you entered his house and saw, to right and left, large, well-lighted display cases containing a collection of the very best fishing rods and reels. But I don't think he ever used any of them.

"He kept a fifty-foot boat under a hangar next to the stables, and he was always carrying out modifications to it, from keel to masthead. It was there for years. The stables were perhaps the most extraordinary sight at Molsheim; they were kept as spick and span as the finest drawingroom, and all the doors were of highly polished wood of the best quality. The stalls were impeccable and were divided by plaited straw matting. Bugatti had some lovely horses, one of them being the tallest thoroughbred known. I really think he liked them better than he did cars.

"Nearby was a riding ring. Wearing a yellow or brown bowler, whip in hand, he would lead his guest to the center of it while stable lads brought out his best horses and walked them round, for his and his guest's entertainment. This performance, which lasted about half an hour, always ended with four Shetland ponies galloping round the sawdust ring like clowns.

"Bugatti also found expression for his original ideas within the house. He was always wanting to change the shape of household things which most of us accept without question. The beds were of special dimensions made to his design by his carpenters, and they were like no other beds ever seen. Even the shoes which were made for him had something out of the ordinary about them.

"He kept a very good table and had several Italian cooks, for he liked Italian cooking best. All the ingredients which went into the dishes were specially chosen and came from all parts of France and Europe. He expected to be able to lunch or dine at any hour of the day—and he kept very irregular hours.

"The shoot he had beyond the factory served him more as an experimental ground for his mechanical gadgets than for sport. I remember that he was always followed by a mule wearing a special harness made to carry four guns (all different), and he used to try them in turn to judge their respective qualities. Then, at lunchtime, a tractor would appear hauling a huge caravan which was fitted out as a dining car; the table was in the form of a narrow, elongated horseshoe. And so he was able to offer his guests lunch at the time and place of deciding that the moment had come to turn to another form of pastime.

"Even a bad motoring accident, which kept him in a hospital at Strasbourg for a time (and where, incidentally, he formed a life-long friendship with Professor Leriche), led him to take an interest in surgical instruments; and he later made improved versions of those used in trepanning.

"I was almost forgetting his interest in motor cars! He was very fond of driving you through out-of-the-way parts of lovely Alsace, which he knew so well, and more often than not it was along lanes which were hardly fit for cars. If my memory serves me right, it was after one of these rides, during which the exhaust pipe of a new model had kept hitting the ground, that he decided to raise the chassis of future models slightly higher from the ground.

"But this material side was only part of the man. His conversation bubbled with ideas which seemed unusual but proved to be practicable, and which were sparked off by anything and everything. I remember him reading an article in L'Illustration about the first Micheline railcars. He at once expressed his admiration for this new form of transport, followed by a running commentary on the improvements, and even changes, that could be made to them. And it was not long before he carried them out, applied to his own railcars.

"In addition to his technical knowledge, he had a most extraordinary instinct about mechanics which saved him hours of calculation. One day, an engineer showed him a part intended for a new model of racing car. Bugatti looked at it for a few moments, then said that one of its supports seemed a bit weak. To which the engineer replied: 'That's exactly why I've brought it to you. That gave 'way during a test this morning.'

"These are only small matters, which may not throw much new light on Ettore Bugatti. However, I thought that by describing some of the lesser-known sides of his character and his extraordinary personality, I might give a truer idea of him to those who did not have the privilege of knowing him."

CHAPTER **17**

THE "BUGATTISTS"

This chapter is a kind of postscript—or perhaps a prolongation of the life described in this biography. It has been said earlier that the "Bugattists" were sportsmen and not concerned with material gain. A cup or some other trophy as a souvenir of a win was the sole ambition of every amateur racing driver, in spite of the risks they took and the considerable expense incurred. They were proud of even the slightest success, which was considered an encouragement for everyone.

This spirit led to the formation of groups of enthusiastic Bugatti customers, who met to exchange views, to celebrate successes and to combine forces for fresh activities.

One evening in 1929, three gentlemen met in London over a glass of beer. Two were smoking pipes and the other, a cigarette. One pipe belonged to D. B. Madley (the first owner of a Crossley-Bugatti, the early Brescia model, made in England just after the First World War under license, and which brought such credit to the firm). The other pipe belonged to Colonel Giles, and the cigarette was being smoked by T. Ambrose Varley. Out of the blueish smoke curling to the ceiling from the two placid pipes and the lively cigarette, the Bugatti Owners' Club came into being.[1] It was officially founded on March 4, 1930.

(1) This is the reason for the picture on the cover of *Bugantics*, the club's journal.

At that time, the idea of forming clubs was not as prevalent as it is now, but this initiative met with immediate response. A committee was formed which undertook the organization and administration of the club, with the threefold object of racing, distributing the latest information on the Bugatti firm and collecting designs and photographs of all the Bugatti models. This was how *Bugantics* came to possess the most complete archives and best documentation on the Molsheim factory and its production, for most of the documents and files at the factory itself were lost during the two World Wars.

Among the members of this first committee were Colonel G. M. Giles and Mr. Eric Giles (chairman at the time of writing), who were both old friends of the Guv'nor.

The first chairman, Earl Howe, asked Ettore Bugatti to be President of the club, on August 10, 1931. Bugatti was very touched by this gesture, which he always considered a great honor.

Two of the earliest members of the club were Jean Bugatti (elected on July 27, 1930) and Colonel W. F. Sorel, an ex-Indian Army officer and manager of the London branch of the Bugatti firm. This was in fact the sole branch, for the firm had only agencies in other countries.

The Guv'nor followed the activities of the club with great interest and pride, valuing its high standards and the enthusiasm of so many customers. The club kept in close touch with the methods of tuning up racing and touring cars at Molsheim, and this knowledge was put into practice at rallies and hill-climbs, especially those held at Prescott and Shelsley Walsh.[1]

___

(1) A passage in *Bugantics* (Vol. 1, No. 7, p. 4) described Jean Bugatti's practice run at Shelsley Walsh the day before a race, in a Type 53 with four-wheel drive: ". . . but had the infernal bad luck to crash! The performance of the car was terrific and it would have undoubtedly beaten the record of Von Stuck by some seconds if it had run on Saturday!"

In 1932, Jean Bugatti was given special permission by his father to enter the Midland Automobile Club's event, and he won the Annual Open hill-climb: "Shelsley Walsh, fastest time, sports cars—Class 5 (special award)—Jean Bugatti."

This gave him great pleasure.[1] He never failed to attend the Prescott meeting, which was followed with much interest by those at Molsheim. The Guv'nor encouraged these races by entering one or two cars of his official team, and he always studied the results very closely.

The Bugatti Owners' Club began to hold an annual "Dinner and Dance" at a well-known London hotel.[2] It was customary to have a Bugatti on display, standing on a platform at one end of the room, polished to shine like new. At some time between the dessert, the speeches and dancing, members of the committee would start up the engine and the room would be filled with noise and the familiar fumes, reviving memories and evoking the thrills and keen contests of the racetrack.

A remarkable thing was that none of those gathered together in honor of this original car ever had any nationalistic feelings because it was a foreign make—perhaps because it was also considered a work of art.

Similar attitudes exist in other countries, such as the United States, Germany and Holland, where flourishing Bugatti Clubs have been formed.

The quarterly publication of the British Bugatti Club has the word *Bugantics* printed diagonally across its front page, together with the Bugatti radiator, the club tie in the

(1) The future of the factory lay in Jean Bugatti, as already explained, and his responsibilities precluded his taking risks. Yet it was while testing the 3.3-litre car entered for the La Baule Grand Prix that he met his death on August 11, 1939.

(2) Now a "Lunch and Prizes," at which trophies won during the year are presented.

Bugatti colors and a Bugatti racing car. It is an interesting, well-illustrated magazine that keeps its readers well posted on activities and developments at the Molsheim factory, and also contains advertisements for the sale or exchange of cars.[1]

In 1937 the Bugatti Owners' Club purchased the estate of Prescott House in order to organize its own competitions. Prescott is in the beautiful Cotswold country close to Cleeve Hill, about five miles from Cheltenham and ninety miles from London. At the top of the hill is the delightful house, and in the grounds is the lovely wrought-iron "Memorial Gate" which was put up in memory of Ettore and Jean Bugatti.

The gradient of the 1,127-yard course is one in twenty, and the cars are timed electrically. Spectators and competitors are well cared for in the matter of refreshment rooms, toilet facilities and cloakrooms.

In 1931 Ettore Bugatti gave a Challenge Trophy for the competitor who had gained the highest overall points in club events during the year.

At the annual dinner in February, 1939, Jean Bugatti announced that he and his father were presenting a Type 51, 2.3-litre twin-cam Grand Sports to the club, for the use of members with no racing car of their own, but who would like to compete in the club events. This gift was much appreciated. But there was so much rivalry over who should have the use of the car, and its allocation was such a difficult matter, that the committee took advantage of the outbreak of war to sell the car, which had only been raced twice.

Five meetings a year are usually held at Prescott, mainly in May and September, when other well-known makes are invited to take part, so that the events are almost on a national scale. In addition, a Concours d'Elégance takes place at Whitsun.

---

(1) The B.O.C. now has a membership of one thousand, of whom two hundred are Bugatti owners.

The Guv'nor gave the "Jean Bugatti Trophy" in memory of his son. It is awarded for the best time by a Bugatti in any competition, either organized by the club or another organization in England or abroad. The Trophy is the property of the Bugatti Owners' Club, but a replica is given annually to the successful contestant.

After Ettore Bugatti's death in Paris on August 21, 1947, Bugatti Clubs were formed in other countries despite the post-war difficulties. The Guv'nor's personality had always brimmed over beyond his purely professional activities, and these clubs were centers where his spirit lived on. Many members have made considerable financial sacrifice and showed infinite patience in restoring vintage Bugatti cars to their original condition.[1] There could be no more touching tribute to a great and honorable man.

In Holland, a keen motorist and sportsman, Wilhelm Prick of Maestricht, the owner of several vintage Bugattis of different types, founded the Netherlands Bugatti Club in October, 74B-1956,[2] on the Zandveert circuit near Amsterdam. Among the Bugattis brought to the meeting were the following types: Type 43, Grand Sports; Type 43, Roadster; Type 40, Grand Sports; Type 40, Roadster.

The committee at the time of writing is as follows:

Chairman	Mr. Wilhelm Prick
Secretary	Dr. Eggy J. de Flines
Treasurer	Dr. Emile J. Burnaby Lautier
Members	Mr. Willen H. Pieters and Mr. Arie M. van Ramshordt.

(1) An interesting letter on this subject is reproduced on a later page, by permission of the American Bugatti Club.

(2) It was Mr. Prick's idea to precede the year by the age that Ettore Bugatti would have had if still living. For instance, he would have been 74 in 1956, so—74B-1956.

I should like to quote from a letter sent to me by the Netherlands Bugatti Club in May, 80B-1962:

"There are fifty-four Bugatti cars in Holland, but not all are in working order. The N.B.C. is composed of a select band of '*Pur-sang* Bugattists' and of 'Bugattists.' Our first aim is to pay tribute to the dear, late Guv'nor, the genius that was Ettore Bugatti, and to his son Jean; second, to recover and restore to their original condition the Guv'nor's creations.

"Each year the N.B.C. organizes two national rallies, in May and September. We have a meeting every so often, when we talk about our dear old Bugattis and show films.

"I have organized big international events—the Grand International Rally (Ermenonville-Le Mans) in 76B-1958, and the Grand International Bugatti Rally (Charleville-Molsheim) in 79B-1961.

"The international events always start from Neer-Canne castle, near Maestricht.

"My friend Herr Kurt Kiefer, an ardent Bugattist of Duisburg, Germany, and Herr Wolfgang Schmarbick of Dusseldorf, organized the Internationale Bugatti Treffen in 78B at Bad-Nonnel; and this year, 80B, there is to be the Internationale Bugatti Treffen at Diez an der Lahn, from the 22nd to the 25th of June. A select band from my club, together with Bugattist friends from Belgium, France and Britain, will set off at 10 a.m. on June 22nd from Neer-Canne castle. I have already mapped out a picturesque route through Germany (Eupen-Montjoie-Coblentz-Rhine bridge-Bad Ems-Nassau) to Diez an der Lahn, which we expect to reach late on the afternoon of June 22nd.

"We have recently made contact with two Bugattists in Japan. A Polish Bugattist, Tadeusz Tabenski of Warsaw, was very sorry to have missed the Grand Rally at Molsheim last year. I have also made contact with Mrs. Elisabeth Junek of Prague.

"My friend Karel Sauerbier of Rotterdam and I are the most active Bugattists in Holland. We were driving Bugattis as far back as 1930, or in 48B."

One of the most exciting events was the Grand International Rally, Maestricht-Charleville-Molsheim, organized in July, 79B-1961, by the Netherlands Bugatti Club. About fifty Bugatti cars of all types took part, coming from England, Denmark, Norway and other countries. One car had made the long and difficult journey from Johannesburg.

The Bugatti family and factory gave these unusual visitors a very warm welcome. The whole town was beflagged, and the Mayor of Molsheim, M. Meck, who was also a county councillor, gave a reception in the old town hall, which was opened for the occasion. A score of young waitresses were dressed in Alsatian costume, and the town band was in attendance. Each of the leading members of the N.B.C. was presented with an etching of the town hall (listed as an historic monument and the pride of the local inhabitants) and wives were given bouquets of summer flowers. In his speech, the Mayor expressed the gratitude that the people of the district felt to Ettore Bugatti for the contribution his factory had made to its economic prosperity.

The rally drivers then proceeded to the factory canteen, which was decorated with the national flags, where 230 people sat down to lunch. Although many of them could only communicate by gestures, because of the language barrier, they all had a common link in their possession of a Bugatti.

It was very touching to see the pride and joy of some of the older workmen as they inspected those chassis and engines, recognizing the work of their own hands; and how they enjoyed hearing the loud throbbing of all those engines, the acceleration and braking along the winding paths round the factory buildings, not to mention the ineffable smells from the exhausts!

After visiting the workshops, all present made their way to the nearby cemetery and gathered round the Bugatti family vault. The *curé* of Dorlisheim said a prayer, and the Mayor of Molsheim and Mr. Prick laid wreaths on behalf of the townspeople and the N.B.C.

In the evening a dinner and dance at the canteen brought the visitors and the factory staff together again, and so ended in friendly, lively manner a great day which will be long remembered by all.

In the spring of 1960, Mr. O. A. (Bunny) Phillips founded the American *Pur-sang* Bugatti Club at San Gabriel, California.

The officials were:

President	O. A. (Bunny) Phillips
Vice-president	Robert A. Day
Secretary and Editor	Robert E. Hammel
Treasurer	Bob Estes
Acting president	Otto Zipper

The aims and statutes of the club are similar to those of the Bugatti Owners' Club in London, but it is run on different lines and has a flavor of its own. The membership is drawn from various countries and already exceeds sixty; the club helps Bugattists to get in touch with one another and to exchange information and even confidences.

For instance, the club's quarterly magazine published the following in its spring, 1961, issue:

"One of the most interesting aspects of the task of editing this magazine is the letters received from all parts of the world, and the devotion they show to the Marque is really fine. The following letter from an owner in Madrid, Spain, is a good example. It is printed just as received, for it seems so very interesting."

Dear Sir,

I am writing to you because I am the happy possessor of a 1926 Bugatti Brescia, chassis no. 2544-48. I have completely restored it to its original condition. But I should like to know the form of the dashboard. If you have a photograph of it, would you be kind enough to send me one? The car was found in a garden at Grenada, where it had been standing in the open for four years. I bought this Brescia and sent it by train to Madrid, where my friends and I cleaned it up, changed the electric wiring, charged the old battery instead of waiting to put in a new one, and after having cleaned the carbureter and the petrol-tank (which were covered with mold), we tried to start up this wonderful 16-valve engine. At the second attempt, it started up! This was amazing! A month later we had got the car into good order, for it was not used to being looked after!

The radiator had a horrible bonnet of aerodynamic design! The car is very handsome now, but the wheels are not of the "Rudge" type. If you wish, I could send you a photo for your magazine.

I am also the founder of the Classic Car and Veteran Club of Madrid. We will keep you informed of our activities. Two of our members own a Type 35 and a Type 39 Bugatti, the Grand Prix model. My brother and I have a Type 60 Bugatti, but without its chassis and not in working order. However, we intend to restore it.

I should like to have news from you.

With many thanks,

Yours sincerely,

Jose Manuel Rodriguez Vina.
Hnos-Alverez Quintoro, 2,
Madrid, Spain.

There is also a German Bugatti Club which is very active. In June, 1962, twenty-nine Bugattis took part in a very successful rally.

The memory of Ettore Bugatti and his work remains alive through these Clubs. He was a creator and a humanist before he was an industrialist, and then he showed himself to be an astute and sometimes wily businessman, conducting the affairs of his factory with success despite keen competition, financial difficulties and the destruction of two wars.

His foresight of things to come can be discerned in many of his mechanical inventions, so that he still exerts a certain fascination. The various active Bugatti Clubs are the most striking proof of this.

THE BUGATTI CIRCUIT AT LE MANS

At a meeting of the Automobile Club de l'Ouest a few years ago it was suggested that a permanent, closed circuit should be created on part of the 24-Hours' open circuit at Le Mans, and that it should be given the name "Bugatti Circuit." It could be used for testing and preparing racing cars throughout the year, without interfering with the road traffic along the main circuit.

The suggestion was approved, and work began on the circuit early in 1964. The news was received with delight and pride by the Bugatti family, needless to say, as well as by Bugatti enthusiasts all over the world.

The Bugatti Circuit is now completed, and makes use of the pits, offices, electrical-timing system, etc., of the Le Mans 24-Hours' circuit. Its length is nearly 5,000 yards. It takes in a part of the 24-Hours' circuit, notably the sharp bend by the Dunlop Bridge (see sketch). The width of the track is thirty feet throughout its length. It is built partly on the Butte Rouge slope, which gives a wide view of the rest of the track.

All the racing drivers and technicians who have used the circuit are agreed that it provides all one could wish for in the way of speed and safety. The object of the Automobile Club de l'Ouest in creating the Bugatti Circuit has been to aid motor racing in general, by providing facilities for car manufacturers to test their models and, especially, for amateur drivers to practice their favorite sport.

There is to be a Driving School which will have at its disposal several different sports cars and racing cars; and lessons based on special methods will be available to drivers wishing to perfect their techniques.

THE BUGATTI CIRCUIT DRIVING SCHOOL

Theory will be taught in addition to the actual driving lessons given during each course. For instance, lectures will be given on the factors governing the stability of a vehicle, with special emphasis on the requisite conditions in order not to upset those factors.

Drivers who attend the course will therefore be well equipped for engaging in motor racing of all kinds. Although still far from being champions, they will at least have a better chance of winning and, in any case, be running less risk.

Courses are to be given on weekends, followed by a supplementary course lasting several days which, it is hoped, will be attended by past pupils who will give the benefit of their experience.

EPILOGUE

"My friend Bugatti," by Gabriel Voisin

There can be no better ending to this book than the moving
testimony of friendship that the famous aircraft constructor,
Gabriel Voisin, has written:

"We were both more or less of the same age.

"But Demeter, described by Homer as the greatest of
goddesses, was by his cradle on September 15, 1881, and
bestowed all her gifts on him.

"I do not remember the occasion of our first meeting. I
seem to have known this amazing engineer all my life, for
Bugatti was already one of us in the pioneering days of
aviation.

"In about 1908, our laboratory was on the Quai du Point-
du-Jour, in Paris, and there he used to visit us once a week.
I always kept our mechanical problems for that friendly
occasion. There seemed to be no snags or obstacles for that
extraordinary man. One had only to state the problem for
it to be solved.

"Many sports writers in these needy days have turned to
the productions of the Molsheim factory for a subject, but
none of these well-informed men has given us a faithful picture of the real Bugatti. Some have recalled his charm,
others have disclosed his whims.

"None of them has seemed able to bring to life this great

man of 'transport,' for the immense talent of this born engineer, this scientific conjurer, was concealed beneath a cloak
of fun and gaiety, and he gave the impression of never taking
himself seriously.

"I am now eighty-six, and in these last years of my life I
can look back and measure the worth of the men I have
known in the course of a career full of surprises.

"Most of my contemporaries were incapable of making an
effort beyond what was required of them by circumstances.
I have therefore very vivid recollections of those few who
were capable of voluntary actions and initiative.

"In his book *The Revolt of the Masses,* José Ortega y
Gasset wrote these inspired words: 'A human life, by its
very nature, has to be devoted to something or other, to a
glorious or humble enterprise, an illustrious or obscure
destiny. This is a strange but inexorable condition of
things.'

"Ortega y Gasset must have known Bugatti at the time of
writing those lines.

"About the year 1908, my old friend had a passion for
steam-driven vehicles. He had a collection of forgotten
masterpieces of absolute silence and instant power; and as I,
too, had a weakness for steam-driven vehicles, this common
interest drew us together.

"The production of cars at Molsheim was really just a
game to my friend, and his successes came easy to him. He
was, however, one of the last car manufacturers able to imagine 'whole,' to assemble in his mind the most varied and
complicated mechanical constructions, effortlessly yet with
exactness.

"In a word, Ettore Bugatti was one of the last mechanics
truly worthy of the name. A large volume would be needed
in order to give a full and clear account of his influence on
'the Wheel.' His cars are well known, but his masterly con-
tributions to light rail locomotion are practically forgotten.

"Before the Second World War, railcars were popularly called 'Bugattis.' After the war, this truly French technician was the victim of regrettable incidents and his health was thereby affected. He passed away in 1947.

"In 1913 I lost my brother Charles in a car accident for which a third party was entirely to blame. He was only thirty, but if he caught a glimpse of the sinister old man with a sickle he must have found death to be kind. He was at the wheel of a Bugatti."

APPENDIX I

The 74 Types of Cars Built at Molsheim

YEAR	TYPE	BORE AND STROKE	NO. OF CYLINDERS	CAPACITY	SPEED IN MPH.
1899					

DESCRIPTION: Tricar entered for the Paris-Bordeaux race, 24th May, 1899.

1899					

DESCRIPTION: Four-engine light car built at Milan; two engines at the front, two at the rear.

1901		90 x 120	4	3 l.	40

DESCRIPTION: Car exhibited at Milan. Weight, 13 cwt.

1902		114 x 130	4	5.3 l.	

DESCRIPTION: 50 HP De Dietrich car, should have taken part in the Paris-Madrid race, but driving-seat too low.

1903		130 x 140	4	7.5 l.	

DESCRIPTION: De Dietrich model.

1904		140 x 160	4	9 l.	

DESCRIPTION: Hermes-Simplex model built at Graffenstaden. 60 and 90 HP. Chain driven; Bosch magneto.

1907		150 x 150	4	10 l.	

DESCRIPTION: Deutz car, overhead camshaft, magneto, 4-speed, chain driven.

1908		62 x 100	4	1,100 cc.	50

DESCRIPTION: Light car prototype built privately by Bugatti at Cologne. Weight, 6 cwt.

1909		95 x 120	4	3.2 l.	

DESCRIPTION: Deutz car, overhead camshaft, two valves per cylinder, shaft-driven.

YEAR	TYPE	BORE AND STROKE	NO. OF CYL- INDERS	CAPACITY	SPEED IN MPH.
1910	13	65 x 100	4	1.4 l.	

DESCRIPTION: Shaft-driven overhead camshaft, two valves per cylinder.

YEAR	TYPE	BORE AND STROKE	NO. OF CYL- INDERS	CAPACITY	SPEED IN MPH.
1911		55 x 90	4	850 cc.	50

DESCRIPTION: Baby Peugeot. 10 HP, 2,000 rpm. Contract signed 16th November, 1911.

1913		100 x 160	4	5 l.	100

DESCRIPTION: 100 HP car (Roland Garros). Overhead camshaft, three valves per cylinder, chain driven.

1913		65 x 100	8	2.7 l.	100

DESCRIPTION: Two engines coupled in tandem.

1914		100 x 180	4	5.65 l.	112

DESCRIPTION: Indianapolis type, overhead camshaft.

1914	22	65 x 100	4	1.4 l.	62

DESCRIPTION: Two valves per cylinder, 4-speed gearbox, reversed springs.

1914	25/26	68 x 108	4	1.57 l.	62

DESCRIPTION: Two valves per cylinder.

1919	22/23	68 x 100		1.5 l.	75

DESCRIPTION: Four valves per cylinder.

1922	13	69 x 100	4	1.5 l.	90

DESCRIPTION: Brescia type, 16-valve, 4-speed gearbox, shaft-driven; twin, dash mounted magnetos.

1917		120 x 160	8	14.4 l.	

DESCRIPTION: 250 HP aeroengine, produced by Diatto and Delaunay.

1918		120 x 160	16	29 l.	

DESCRIPTION: 16-cylinder double-bank aeroengine, 500 HP, two crankshafts. Purchased by U.S. Government.

YEAR	TYPE	BORE AND STROKE	NO. OF CYL-INDERS	CAPACITY	SPEED IN MPH.
1922	28	69 x 100	8	3 l.	

DESCRIPTION: The first straight-eight Bugatti, gearbox in rear axle.

1922	29/30	60 x 88	8	2 l.	75

DESCRIPTION: Improved version of Type 28. The famous 2 and 2.3 litre racing-cars were based upon this model.

1923	32	60 x 88	8	2 l.	110

DESCRIPTION: Type 30 engine, gearbox in rear axle, racing-car with "tank" body, successful in Tours Grand Prix. Front hydraulic brakes.

1924	33	60 x 88	8	2 l.	

DESCRIPTION: Tourer, with gearbox in rear axle (but was never produced, being replaced by the Type 38).

1924	34	125 x 130	16	25 l.	

DESCRIPTION: Aeroengine with two crankshafts, two straight-eight cylinders. All the Royale cars were given this straight-eight engine, as were the Bugatti railcars, with certain modifications. Some of the railcar engines ran for 75,000 to 90,000 miles without needing to be taken down and over-hauled.

1924	35	60 x 88	8	2 l.	110 plus

DESCRIPTION: Racing-car with many new features: wheels of light alloy, hollow front axle, brake drums, roller bearing crankshaft. Most successful of Bugatti racing-cars for several years. The following modifications were made in 1926: stroke increased to 100 mm.; supercharged engine.

Other versions of Type 35 were:

	35A	60 x 88	8	2 l.	93

DESCRIPTION: Unblown racing-car.

YEAR	TYPE	BORE AND STROKE	NO. OF CYL- INDERS	CAPACITY	SPEED IN MPH.
	35B	60 x 100	8	2.3 l.	125

DESCRIPTION: Supercharged racing-car, aluminum wheels.

| | 35C | 60 x 88 | 8 | 2 l. | 125 |

DESCRIPTION: Supercharged racing-car, aluminum wheels.

| | 35T | 60 x 100 | 8 | 2.3 l. | 112 |

DESCRIPTION: Unblown racing-car, aluminum wheels.

| 1926 | 36 | 51.3 x 66 | 8 | 1.1 l. | |

DESCRIPTION: Single-seater, supercharged 8-cylinder engine (Alsace Grand Prix, 1926).

| 1925 | 37 | 69 x 100 | 4 | 1.5 l. | 93 |

DESCRIPTION: Unblown racing-car. Supercharged version was type 37A.

| 1926 | 38 | 60 x 88 | 8 | 2 l. | 75 |

DESCRIPTION: Modified Type 30 engine. Supercharged version was Type 38A.

| 1926 | 39A | 51.3 x 66 | 8 | 1,493 cc. | |
| 1926 | 39B | 52 x 88 | 8 | 1.5 l. | 125 |

DESCRIPTION: Supercharged racing-car, derivative Type 35.

1926	39C	54 x 81	8	1.5 l.	
1926	39D	51.3 x 66	8	1.5 l.	
1926	40	69 x 100	4	1.5 l.	75

DESCRIPTION: Tourer with Type 37 engine.

| 1930 | 40A | 72 x 100 | 4 | 1.63 l. | 75 |

DESCRIPTION: Same as above, but bore enlarged to 72 mm.

| 1925– | 41 | 125 x 130 | 8 | 12.8 l. | 120 |

DESCRIPTION: The famous Royale.

| 1927 | 42 | 125 x 160 | 8 | 15.8 l. | |

YEAR	TYPE	BORE AND STROKE	NO. OF CYL-INDERS	CAPACITY	SPEED IN MPH.

DESCRIPTION: Engine to be used in a ship which would cross the Atlantic in fast time, but this idea never got beyond the design stage. A model of the ship still exists.

| 1927 | 43 | 60 x 100 | 8 | 2.3 l. | 100 |

DESCRIPTION: Supercharged 2/4-seater sports car, of which Charles Faroux said: "One is sorry to have to stop for petrol, so easy is it to drive."

| 1927 | 44 | 69 x 100 | 8 | 3 l. | 80 |

DESCRIPTION: Tourer, derivative Type 28 engine.

| 1928 | 45 | 60 x 84 | 16 | 3.8 l. | 125 |

DESCRIPTION: Two-seater Grand Sports, two straight-eight supercharged engines, two crankshafts.

| 1929 | 46 | 81 x 130 | 8 | 5.35 l. | 93 |

DESCRIPTION: The last tourer designed by Bugatti. Single overhead camshaft, three valves per cylinder, gearbox in rear axle.

| 1929 | 47 | 60 x 66 | 16 | 3 l. | 125 |

DESCRIPTION: Two-seater Grand Sports, derivative Type 45.

| 1930 | 48 | 60 x 88 | 4 | 1,000 cc. | |

DESCRIPTION: Supercharged 4-cylinder engine, delivered to Peugeot.

| 1930 | 49 | 72 x 100 | 8 | 3.3 l. | 80 |

DESCRIPTION: Tourer, derivative Type 44 engine.

| 1930 | 50 | 86 x 107 | 8 | 4.9 l. | 110 |

DESCRIPTION: Sports/racing-car, twin overhead camshaft, supercharged engine.

| 1930 | 50T | 86 x 107 | 8 | 4.9 l. | 100 |

DESCRIPTION: Tourer version of above.

The Royale, with the first body designed by Jean Bugatti. (*Mlle. Bugatti*)

Jean Bugatti.
(*Mlle. Bugatti*)

The first Royale, with a Packard body. Bugatti drove it on its first test run, so impatient was he to try it out. (*Mlle. Bugatti*)

Type 101, Ettore Bugatti's last production. (*H. G. Conway*)

Mr. C. A. Chayne with his Royale (coachwork by Weinberger of Munich).
(*Jacques Rousseau*)

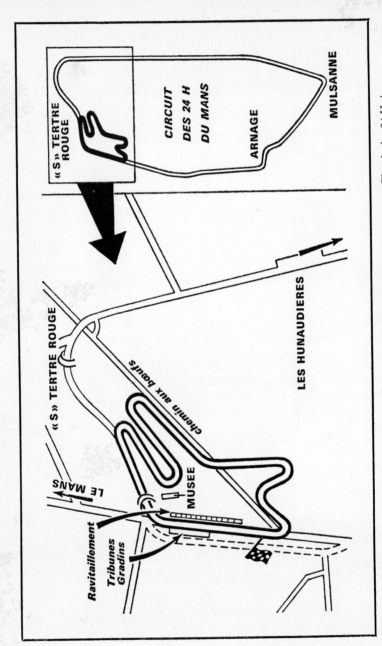

The Bugatti Circuit. (Tribunes=stands, ravitaillement=pits, musee=museum, Circuit des 24 H du Mans=The Le Mans 24-Hours' Circuit.)

YEAR	TYPE	BORE AND STROKE	NO. OF CYL- INDERS	CAPACITY	SPEED IN MPH.
1930	51	60 x 100	8	2.3 l.	135

DESCRIPTION: Racing-car, Type 35 derivative, twin-cam supercharged engine.

1927	52				15

DESCRIPTION: Half-scale model of Type 35 racing-car for children, electrically propelled, 12-volt accumulator, 4-wheel brakes, aluminum wheels.

1931	53	86 x 107	8	4.9 l.	125

DESCRIPTION: Type 50 engine, 4-wheel drive, independently sprung front wheels.

1932	54	86 x 107	8	4.9 l.	150

DESCRIPTION: Type 50 engine, G.P. chassis. World's Hour Record, 134 mph., driven by Czaykowsky at Avus in 1933.

1931	55	60 x 100	8	2.3 l.	112

DESCRIPTION: Twin-cam super-sports, two-seater roadster body, supercharged Type 51 engine. In October, 1932, was driven from Molsheim to Paris in 3 h. 47 mins.

1928	56				20

DESCRIPTION: Two-seater electric runabout.

1932	57	72 x 100	8	3.3 l.	93

DESCRIPTION: Twin-cam tourer.

1934	58	115 x 130	8	10.4 l.	

DESCRIPTION: Supercharged Diesel engine.

1933	59	72 x 100	8	3.3 l.	130

DESCRIPTION: Supercharged, racing chassis.

1933	60	86 x 88	8	4.1 l.	

DESCRIPTION: Aeroengine, four valves per cylinder.

1935	57S	72 x 100	8	3.3 l.	125

DESCRIPTION: Sports chassis.

YEAR	TYPE	BORE AND STROKE	NO. OF CYL- INDERS	CAPACITY	SPEED IN MPH.
1935	57SC	72 x 100	8	3.3 l.	135

DESCRIPTION: Supercharged, sports chassis.

1936	57G	72 x 100	8	3.3 l.	140

DESCRIPTION: 24-Hours' and G.P. chassis.

1936	57S/45	84 x 107	8	4.7 l.	130

DESCRIPTION: Racing-car, Type 50B engine.

1938	57C	72 x 100	8	3.3 l.	75

DESCRIPTION: Supercharged tourer.

1937	50B	84 x 107	8	4.7 l.	

DESCRIPTION: Supercharged racer.

1937	50B	84 x 100	8	4.5 l.	

DESCRIPTION: Unblown racer.

1937	50B	84 x 107	8	4.7 l.	83

DESCRIPTION: Speed-boat engine, world record 83 mph.

1938	50B/111	78 x 78	8	3 l.	

DESCRIPTION: Compound cylinder block, steel sleeve valves, two superchargers.

1938	50B	84 x 107	8	4.7 l.	

DESCRIPTION: Supercharged aeroengine.

1938	50B	84 x 107	8	4.7 l.	

DESCRIPTION: Engine intended for motor launch to have eight engines and four propellers.

1938–39	61, 62, 63				

DESCRIPTION: Various experimental designs.

1938	64	84 x 100	8	4.5 l.	

DESCRIPTION: Car intended for the 1939 Paris Motor Show, called the Jean Bugatti car.

YEAR	TYPE	BORE AND STROKE	NO. OF CYL- INDERS	CAPACITY
1940	65			

DESCRIPTION: Experimental monoblock engine.

| 1938–39 | 66 | | | |

DESCRIPTION: Light plane with two propellers.

| 1939 | 67 | | | |

DESCRIPTION: 16-cylinder aeroengine, experimental.

| 1942 | 68 | 48.5 x 50 | 4 | 37 cc. |

DESCRIPTION: Prototype, twin-cam supercharged 4-cylinder engine.

| | 69 | (no record) | | |
| 1942 | 70 | | | |

DESCRIPTION: Four 4-cylinder engines in X-form.

| 1942 | 71 | 140 x 150 | 8 | 18.5 l. |

DESCRIPTION: Experimental engine.

| 1943 | 72 | 24 x 28 | 1 | 12.7 cc. |

DESCRIPTION: Bicycle motor.

| 1943 | 73 | 70 x 95 | 4 | 1.45 l. |

DESCRIPTION: Four valves inclined at 70 degrees, twin-camshafts.

| 1943 | 73A | 76 x 82 | 4 | 1.48 l. |

DESCRIPTION: Three vertical valves, supercharged, overhead camshaft.

| 1943 | 73B | 76 x 82 | 4 | 1.48 l. |

DESCRIPTION: Three vertical valves.

| 1946 | 73C | 70 x 95 | 4 | 1.46 l. |

DESCRIPTION: Four valves inclined at 70 degrees, supercharged, twin-camshafts.

YEAR	TYPE	BORE AND STROKE	NO. OF CYL-INDERS	CAPACITY
1945	74	170 x 180	2	

DESCRIPTION: Steam-driven.

| 1944 | 75 | 60 x 60 | 1 | 170 cc. |

DESCRIPTION: Single-cylinder engine for boat named *You-You*.

| 1944 | 76 | | | 5 l. |

DESCRIPTION: Lorry engine.

| 1945 | 77 | | | |

DESCRIPTION: Reverse gear, 100 HP.

| 1946 | 78 | 82 x 107 | 8 | 4.5 l. |

DESCRIPTION: Car with straight-eight engine, four valves per cylinder, two overhead camshafts.

| 1946 | 79/80 | | | |

DESCRIPTION: Reverse gear, 10 HP.

| 1951 | 101 | 72 x 100 | | 3.3 l. |

DESCRIPTION: Two valves per cylinder.

| 1951 | 101C | 72 x 100 | | 3.3 l. |

DESCRIPTION: Two valves per cylinder.

APPENDIX II

Jean Bugatti's Productions

1930	Type 50	Sports car and racing-car, twin-cam. A Type 50 engine was used in a number of later racing-cars. For instance: Type 53, four-wheel drive; Type 50B, blown and unblown version; the challenger in the "Million" race (1937–39).
		1938: Supercharged engine of speed-boat which established world record of 83 mph. (Levasseur).
		1938–39: Supercharged engines in high-speed plane (De Monge); two engines coupled in tandem and two contra-rotating propellers.
		1938–39: Supercharged engines for motor-torpedo-boat (eight engines and four propellers).
1931	Type 51	Racing-car, 2.3 litre, twin-cam, super-charged. Successor to the famous Type 35. A modified version was the Type 55 super-sports in which Jean Bugatti drove from Molsheim to Paris in 3 hours 47 minutes.
1932–33	Type 57	3.3 liter tourer, twin-cam, 130 HP. Later versions: 57S, sports chassis; 57SC, two- and four-seater; 57G, racing-car, 24-Hours' and Grand Prix.
1936–37	Type 57S/45	Racing-car with Type 50B engine.

1938–39 Type 50B/111	Prototype 8-cylinder 3 litre super-charged engine, bore and stroke 78 x 78, twin-cam, four valves per cylinder. Light alloy.
1938–39 Type 64	8-cylinder 4.5 litre car, 4-speed Cotal gearbox; aluminum engine-block, hydraulic starter.
1927–39	Designed about 110 car bodies, among them being the Atalante coupé, the Stelvio cabriolet, the Galibier and Ventoux saloon.

APPENDIX III

Ettore Bugatti's Yacht

Ettore Bugatti was fond of the sea, and on several occasions he turned his mind to designing and building boats of various tonnage. Towards the end of 1938 he began to make one of his dreams come true—to have a yacht whose construction would benefit from all his knowledge of boat-building and the ideas in this connection which had accumulated over twenty years. Most of these ideas had already been expressed in patents and the construction of various apparatus such as a windlass, capstan, rudder-controls, propeller shafts, etc.

This yacht was laid down in 1939 at the Macario shipyard at Trouville, on the Normandy coast. Its principal characteristics were (approximately):

Length overall—90 feet; waterline length—70 feet; beam—21 feet. Height of masts from deck—115 feet. Sail area—3,000 square feet.

The compartments below deck were: six cabins giving onto a passage-way running fore-and-aft; a dining room or saloon; a cabin aft, which could be used as a saloon; and an engine room.

A cabin amidships, intended for navigation, was to have a metal roof twelve feet by six and glass sides above deck, with glass also set in the deck around it, to light the area below.

The vessel had a wooden hull, and Ettore Bugatti had decided on teak for the deck and the bulwarks.

The ribs were joined to the keel by steel flats. The keel was ballasted with a length of cast-iron weighing about twelve tons and bolted to the keel and the flats.

The sail plan consisted chiefly of a foresail and a mainsail. The foresail was maneuvered by means of a capstan, but the mainsail had a kind of roller-reefing gear specially invented by Bugatti. The sail was rolled around (i.e., taken in or let out) a vertical tube supported by two metal lengths fixed to either bulwark and themselves given additional support by the shrouds. The tube was rotated by a mechanism below deck, and the amount of canvas taken in varied with the number of turns given to the tube.

The mechanism was driven by an electric motor run off the ship's batteries; this turned the tube, or reefing-gear, by means of a reduction gear.

The sail had to be kept stretched tight, whether being taken in or let out; and to this end a nylon cable was sewn to the foot-lining of the sail and ran along the boom, passing over a system of pullies and returning to the reefing mechanism over a drum or windlass.

The windlass tended to turn at a faster rate than the reefing-gear when the sail was being let out, and at a slower rate when it was being taken in, due to friction and the play of the pullies; as a result, there was a pull on the sail towards the stern.

The full details of this gear appear in Bugatti's specifications which he filed on November 5, 1943, although the patent was dated March 14, 1951 (French patent no. 985,485).

Bugatti's inventive genius also extended to the rudder and steering. He introduced a reduction gear between the wheel and the rudder, and the mechanism included a coupling and cogged pinion intended to reduce the shock imparted by the action of the waves. This invention was protected by French patent no. 999,967, dated October 10, 1951 (but filed on February 8, 1946).

The yacht was to have two auxiliary engines, placed aft. Each of these engines (Ford V8) would have a Picker reverse gear, a horizontal shaft driving the dynamos and a vertical shaft to drive the propeller, but by means of a complicated mechanism underneath the hull (French patent no. 842,384, dated March 6, 1939, filed on February 12, 1938).

Ettore Bugatti had in fact thought out the construction and fittings of the yacht down to the smallest details, from the pumps and the winches for raising the anchor to the funiture and even wash-basins. The latter were made at his factory to his own design. An oval table intended for the saloon aft caused a lot of trouble and had to be remade several times, since the shape had to follow the curving sides of the hull.

Unfortunately, the building of the yacht was interrupted by the German invasion of France. It was launched at Easter, 1940, but all work on it came to a halt in May. When the Germans drew near, M. Macario took the hull in tow and got it across the Seine estuary to Le Havre, from where it was got across to England. It remained in a south-coast port throughout the war. The midships cabin had not been completed; and although the deck opening was covered over, some deterioration necessarily occurred—apart from that caused by five or six years in the water.

Ettore Bugatti managed to recover it after the war, and had it brought to the shipyard at Maisons-Lafitte, on the Seine, which he had purchased. With his usual energy, he set about completing the yacht, so far as his numerous other activities would allow. But his serious illness brought his plans to an end, and after his death there was no one in the family with sufficient technical knowledge to take up his plans for the yacht.

Domboy.

APPENDIX IV

Ettore Bugatti's Patents Concerning Speed-boats, Aircraft and Machine-tools

After the First World War, Ettore Bugatti filed a number of patents concerning boat design and propeller shafts.

He fitted engines to several speed-boats, notably:

The *Niniette,* in 1932; this reached a speed of 66 mph. with Prince Ruspoli at the wheel.

In 1936 he built a speed-boat for Piquerez which won a world record with a speed of 83 mph. It was driven by a Type 50B supercharged straight-eight engine (capacity 4.7 litre) and had two propellers in line.

Among other boats built by Ettore Bugatti was a motor-torpedo-boat with a light alloy hull (Duralinox), driven by eight Type 50B engines arranged in two rows.

He filed a number of patents concerning aircraft construction. They dealt in particular with propeller shafts, reverse flow, tail control, engine-cooling systems and contra-rotating propellers.

In 1938 he designed a high-speed, light combat plane. It was expected to attain a speed of 500 mph., which was very fast for that time. The construction was entirely of wood, following the principles in his specifications contained in French patent no. 859,179, dated May 27, 1940. Two contra-rotating propellers drove a pair of shafts from two Type 50B supercharged engines of about 400 HP each. The engines were coupled in tandem, and the pilot's seat was between the two shafts. The exhausts came out each side of the fuselage, the blowers being inboard. The radiator was in the rear fuselage and was fed by reverse flow from air entering the leading edge.

The first test-flight was scheduled for the summer of 1940. The collapse of France in June caused the whole project to be abandoned, when the plane was within a month of completion.

Many of its features represented considerable advance on aeronautical techniques at that time.

During the last years of his life, Ettore Bugatti concentrated his inventive genius on machine-tools, on those used in shipbuilding as well as on those used in car manufacture. The former included machines for bending and shaping steel plates, for chamfering, riveting, etc., while among the latter may be noted the special lathes for manufacturing the Hispano-Suiza crankshafts on which his factory was engaged in 1939–40. But circumstances prevented the development of this new technique. Incidentally, it is noteworthy that the foreign patents protecting this invention were granted after the war, and even as late as June, 1948.

Domboy.

APPENDIX V

Impressions of an Astonishing Automobile Factory in an Alsatian Village

(reprinted from *The Autocar*, Nov. 14, 1930)

by

MAURICE SAMPSON

If you happen to find yourself in the handsome city of Strasbourg, noted, as Michelin truly observes, for *pâtés et terrines de foie gras d'Alsace, et eau-de-vie de fruits,* and you can tear yourself away from these undoubted aids to the joy of living, you can run out a few miles over one of the most perfect bits of speedway I have ever motored on, and soon find yourself on the outskirts of the pleasant, prettily situated village of Molsheim. There are fewer than three thousand inhabitants of this little place, and if you asked them what they did most of their time the great majority of heads of households would answer at once by naming a car known the world over by repute, and "personally" to great numbers of enthusiastic amateurs in the Old World.

INTERNATIONALISM.

But, curiously enough, the feudal lord of Molsheim, that little village in a district which has alternately owed allegiance to France, to Germany and again to France, is one of neither of these countries by birth: he is Italian born, and his name is Ettore Bugatti.

I am fain to confess that, of all the works of which I had ever heard, I had more keen desire to look over the *usines* Bugatti than any others. All sorts of legends have grown up around this remarkable genius. I use the word genius advisedly, for if ever a man had a touch of what Dante termed the divine afflatus Ettore Bugatti is that man.

You can have your own opinion about his cars. You may not like them, or you may love them. But you have to have an opinion. A Bugatti car is not just a nebulous mass of machinery. It is vitally alive. It may not be the last word in silence; it may, indeed, be the last word in noisiness, if a supercharged super sports model; but it is a very compelling car, and its tremendous record of successes proves it has more than pace; it has stoutness and courage. It is, as M. Bugatti would say, *le pur sang*—a thoroughbred. On every race track in the world, at the start of some big event, the question almost always is: "What will the Bugs do?"

So I must be excused if I felt all a flutter when I found myself speeding down the fast leg of the old Strasbourg Grand Prix course towards Molsheim on a beautiful summer morning.

DOMESTICITY.

You come to a spot where at a crossroads there is a gracious house of the sort of which any English country gentleman would approve. It stands in beautiful grounds with restful gardens, above which two or three storks are demonstrating how incredibly graceful an act flying and gliding can be. It is the home of the Bugatti family. Bear round the corner, and here, just at the rear of the gardens, is the entrance to the works. There is a porter's lodge on the right with a weigh-table in front, but the note of tremendous individuality pervading everything is apparent, for the lodge is like a little Roman temple, with a colonnade of pillars in front. It is, of course, designed by the *patron*.

The main shops lie in front of you; a beautiful working room with a drawing office attached is close by. In here the *patron* works, what time he is not riding his horses, designing his carriages, superintending his estate, building a boat, visiting his people, looking after his dogs, or doing any one of a hundred tasks that fall to the lot of a country gentleman of the rather old-time sort.

The fact is, M. Bugatti is the feudal lord of Molsheim, and the villagers look to him and his family for a lead in affairs, for advice in difficulties, for help and sympathy in misfortune. The trust and affection are obviously mutual, and the whole enterprise proves that feudalism, correctly interpreted, is a vital force for goodwill and peace and mutual endeavour. Perhaps a little of the same spirit in my own land would not be amiss in these days.

And the shops! Suppose you were a very wealthy amateur, with a flair for mechanics, and could command the very latest and best in machine tools and mechanics of the type from which racing *équipes* are recruited, you would find your heart's desire if, for instance, the chassis erecting shop at Molsheim were yours.

Everything is done perfectly and in its order. Time is not wasted, naturally, because a good workman does not waste anything, but there is no undue haste. The great thing is not do the job so that it will merely satisfy the *patron,* but so perfectly that it will draw a word of commendation from him. Curiously enough, the only other works in which I have noticed this almost luxurious pride in handiwork, where a file or a scraper is used as only an artist-mechanic can use these very difficult tools, is one in England where the world's best is the ideal to strive for—the Rolls-Royce establishment at Derby.

Rolls-Royce and Bugatti! Strange companions to bracket together! Yet each represents the *ne plus ultra* in its special sphere—perfection in silent touring cars, and the utmost overall efficiency in sporting models. The same extraordinarily fine pride in the skill of the human hand, the same neatness and cleanliness and orderliness in the shops, the same rigid inspection, the same firm refusal to hurry anything, or to market anything of which the firm is likely to be anything but proud, are evident to the observer in both establishments. This is a spirit which, in automobile manufacture, is bound to result in lasting success, and, when practised, stamps indelibly the product with the unmistakable hall-mark of real individuality.

You may search the benches at Molsheim, and never find a file mark on a vise; you will find every machine tool kept as clean and as polished as the part it is making, and you will see hand fitting and finishing of pistons and gudgeon pins, and con-rods and other parts, done with a precision which carried my mind back in a flash over the hundreds of miles to Derby in my native Midlands.

Everyone who really loves good work for its own sake must be sincerely glad that men like Royce and Bugatti are to be numbered among the chiefs of the automobile industry. They not only keep alive good engineering ideals, they inspire ideals in their employees.

I hope no one will mind my coupling these two names. I cannot help it, and that is how it struck me.

I think it is rather a pity that the world at large knows so little of what Bugatti can do and has done in automobile engineering. The name is, in the main, associated with small, highly efficient and noisy sports cars. Why, you may ask, does not this remarkable man devote his talents to the production of quiet cars? The answer is simple. In the past the question of silence had not cropped up with him. The whole aim was overall Efficiency with a capital E. Today, however, Bugatti will give you a very crisp exhaust, or, if you prefer it, he will give you a very silent car with a crisp performance. The new five-litre straight eight is witness, as anyone who knows that exotic car will agree.

Then there is the Gold Bug! There is only one in being, the *patron's* own car. It is a very king among cars, huge, impressive, elegant. It is so big that a Rolls Royce looks small beside it!

But it is definitely in production. I saw over a dozen components' sets passing through the shops; engines and back axies-cum-two-speed-gear boxes. I heard a list of names on the waiting list. One is a ruling monarch, another a great captain of the automobile industry. The Gold Bug is silent. It is said to be capable of 120 mph. in full touring trim. As one of the engineers said to me, "The master turns his attention to silence. We shall make very quiet cars when the master gives the command."

His choice of terms was correct. The *patron* is the master; his wishes are unquestioned commands. Ettore Bugatti knows intimately the history, family associations, peculiarities, special skill or otherwise, of every one of his thousand employees. He knows the name of each, and he is father-confessor, employer, and feudal lord. His men know him, appreciate him and respect him as a man, as an employer, and as a workman.

VERSATILITY.

He can do any job in the factory as well as, or better than, the most skilled mechanic. His mind flits from dog-clutches to dogs—his kennel of English wire-haired terriers is a delight—from horse-power to horses—he has superb examples of blood-stock, hunters, ponies and even a Sicilian donkey, in his beautiful stables built alongside the factory. He has a saddle-room and coach-house that, I think, would please the eye of Lord Lonsdale himself, and right at hand to his drawing office is a great riding school, where he shows that he knows as much of horsemanship as he does of automobile engineering.

He presents a remarkable ensemble, this horse-loving squire who fills in his time making very fast cars. What a pity he was not on some of our own county benches in the early days of motoring in England!

As we are accustomed today to view motor car manufacturing plants, the Bugatti works are quite small. I do not know how many cars they send forth annually; I did not ask. But I do know that the works are superbly equipped as regards vital machine tools, and that the milling, gear cutting, and crankshaft and other grinding cannot be bettered anywhere. There are no awe-inspiring press tools, but there is a very perfect little heat-treatment department, and some notably fine drop forges of the smaller sort, for steering arms and the like, are to be seen.

No! It is the training to perfection of the human hand that strikes one as the paramount feature of the place; that and the general air of artistry over all. For instance, you might think that an ordinary door with ordinary hinges and locks might suffice to give entry to or exit from the shops. If you cherish any such idea you do not know M. Bugatti. Every single door in the factory is of beautiful polished oak, and every hinge is of solid, highly polished brass, and each door has a different Yale lock. The Master holds, as is befitting, the master key. Those doors fascinated me; each was so completely beautiful, nay, magnificent, in itself.

DIVERTISEMENT.

We wandered about in the shops, absorbed by the all too rare sight of men using fine files as fine files are meant to be employed. We flitted from shop to stable, from stable to kennel, from kennel to a boat-building slip. And there we stopped a long time. M. Bugatti has his own ideas on how a cabin cruiser should be designed and fitted up, and he is making a cruiser which, whatever its actual performance, will be a most pleasant and convenient craft in which to voyage. Indeed, I think the perfect summer day would include ideal Vosges weather, a trip to the Rhine in the Gold Bug, and a day on that wonderful river with the *patron* on his finished cruiser. What a life!

Not only the perfection of environment and transport, but I can assure you the commissariat would leave no cause for complaint. And that reminds me, as Alice used to say.

I had quite forgotten two very important details of the *établissement Ettore Bugatti*. Right plump in the centre of the tableau is a beautiful little private distillery wherein are made special ingredients for the cocktail *de la maison,* and just up the road and standing in the grounds of the estate is Bugatti's own inn, the Hôtellerie de Pur Sang.

HOSPITALITY.

You must come along here at lunch time, for not only will you have the warmest of welcomes from the cheery Italian and his capable wife who run the little hotel, but you will be able to drink the famous cocktail, eat some most excellent French food cooked in the Italian manner, and try some notably good local Riesling wine. M. Bugatti maintains the little hotel for the benefit of visitors and clients whose tastes are exceptional, and who prefer the quiet of Molsheim to the stir of Strasbourg. I do not know if he finds hotel-keeping a paying business, but I do know one gets jolly good value for money there. Other manufacturers, please copy!

Well, we all sit and chat after lunch, which includes spaghetti, reminding me of Milan. A brilliant sun is beating down on the myriad chestnut and laburnum blossoms which seem to cover this lovely countryside.

A car comes up, a five-litre, to speed us back along that wonderful stretch of road down which the little red Fiats snaked at almost sickening speed in 1922. The five-litre is very fast, it is also very quiet. As the technician said, the Master is turning his mind to silence.

Yet I, for one, feel rather sorry. Somehow a Bug without a bark would seem so very unreal, and, whatever it is or is not, the Bug is definitely a very, very real motor car.